Bread Machine Cookbook for Beginners:

Unveil the Ancient Art of Bread Making throu
and Easy Recipes with the Magic of Your Baking
[II EDITION]

Copyright © 2023

Sarah Roslin

TABLE OF CONTENTS

1 INTRODUCTION

Creating bread from scratch can be a time-intensive endeavor, but the rewards are manifold, including the enjoyment of wholesome and delectable loaves. The art of bread-making demands a combination of patience, meticulous attention to detail, and dedicated effort. Thankfully, bread machines can shoulder much of this burden, allowing you to concentrate on the delightful end product. Bread machines have emerged as indispensable companions for those who might not possess the time or patience to undergo the traditional, laborious process of hand-making bread. Even though bread is readily available at supermarkets, there is an undeniable charm in crafting your own loaves at home. This not only allows for customization according to personal preferences and nutritional requirements but also ensures the usage of fresh, high-quality ingredients. Enter the bread machine - an ingenious kitchen appliance that streamlines the bread-making process. Resembling an electric countertop oven, this device is specially engineered to bake bread. Its exterior is usually crafted from a material like tin, which maintains an elegant appearance despite housing a powerful electric motor. The motor is connected to an axle, on which a small metal paddle is affixed. This paddle, housed inside the tin, rotates to mix the ingredients. The axle is secured by a waterproof seal to prevent leakage of the bread mixture. Bread, a versatile staple, has traditionally complemented an array of meals, whether breakfast, lunch, or dinner. With a bread machine, you can effortlessly create this essential accompaniment at home while avoiding the artificial additives commonly found in store-bought varieties. This cookbook contains a plethora of recipes to be tried out with your bread machine. Using fresh ingredients, you can indulge in the delightful flavors that homemade bread offers, all while keeping your kitchen free from the clutter of pots and pans.

2 WHAT IS A BREAD MACHINE

A bread machine is an ingenious kitchen appliance designed to simplify the process of making bread. Typically, it consists of a pan or bucket equipped with one or more kneading paddles, which are powered by an electric motor to mix and knead dough to the desired consistency for baking. The pan is often cylindrical in shape to facilitate even rising and browning of the bread.

Bread machines are available in vertical and horizontal configurations. The more prevalent horizontal models are favored by home bakers. In a vertical machine, a single kneading paddle at the bottom of the pan is driven by the electric motor. Horizontal models usually feature two paddles, with one at the top and the other at the bottom. These paddles may turn in opposite directions for effective kneading, although in certain models they may rotate in the same direction, yielding a denser dough and less uniform loaf. Some bread machines boast adjustable kneading paddles to accommodate various bread types. Additionally, if extensive kneading is required, the dough can be removed post-rising for additional kneading in a stand mixer. Bread machines have been gracing our kitchens for several decades, automating tasks such as ingredient mixing, dough kneading and rising, and baking. They also allow for unattended operation, which is particularly convenient for busy individuals.

The Bread Machine Yeast

Bread machines typically employ a special yeast, aptly named Bread Machine Yeast, which enables the baking of an assortment of bread without the need for manual kneading or rising times. The yeast should be combined with flour and added to the bread machine. Unlike traditional methods that require yeast to be dissolved in water, bread machine yeast can be mixed directly with dry ingredients. This yeast has a virtually indefinite shelf life if kept in its original packaging in a cool environment. Yeast is a single-celled organism that multiplies through budding. This multiplication is essential for successful bread-making as it generates carbon dioxide, which causes the dough to rise. However, when the yeast begins to expire, fermentation ceases, and the bread turns stale.

Pros and Cons of a Bread machine

Pros of Bread machine

1. Effortless and efficient bread-making.
2. Tidier and more streamlined compared to traditional methods.
3. Consistent quality and taste with each loaf.
4. Capability to make jams and jellies.
5. No manual kneading required.
6. Customizable with a range of ingredients.
7. Ideal for individuals with busy schedules.
8. Economical in the long run.

Cons of Bread machine

1. The paddle may get stuck in the bread, leaving a hole upon removal.
2. Some models have limitations in terms of programming.
3. Cleaning can be cumbersome.
4. Can consume a significant amount of electricity.
5. Limited lifespan for most models.

3 DIFFERENT TYPES OF BREAD MACHINES

Depending on your family size and baking needs, your choice of bread machine may differ from others. Various machines, through their diverse cycles, can bake a single loaf or multiple loaves.

1. No Kneading Machines - Many newer models eliminate the need for kneading. These machines are perfect if you're baking for your family as they simplify the process.
2. Knead and Rise Machines - These machines are ideal if you're baking a large loaf but wish to avoid using an oven. They allow you to bake up to three loaves simultaneously, but this convenience might come at a higher cost.
3. Knead, Rise, and Bake Machines - These comprehensive machines may be more expensive but can bake up to five loaves at once. They require a certain level of expertise as they don't automate the entire process. If you're seeking a basic machine, this type could be suitable.

The second type of bread machine offers more features than the basic models. These enhancements may include delayed start time, crust color control, temperature regulation, and other features that simplify its use.

The third type is what most people envision when they think of bread machines. These fully automated machines allow you to add your ingredients, press a button, and let it do its magic. They often come with additional features like delayed start time, crust color control, and temperature regulation. Some of these machines even offer single-button operation. However, they tend to be more expensive. These professional-grade bread machines come equipped with all the bells and whistles, including automated paddle stirring, delay time of up to 24 hours, and the ability to bake more than just bread. Due to their complexity, they may not be the best choice for home use. Keep in mind that these machines are quite large, similar to a microwave oven, and may require significant counter space. The price tag can reach into the thousands, but if you plan to bake large amounts of dough regularly, this could be the best option for you.

Why Do Bread Made From Bread Machine Has Similar Taste To Bread Made By Hands And Oven

Bread made with a bread machine tastes remarkably similar to hand-made bread due to several factors. One reason is the addition of yeast flakes to the dough. When yeast cells rupture, they merge with the starch granules, enhancing the texture of the bread. Mechanical mixing of dough in a bread machine also leads to a more even distribution of air bubbles compared to hand mixing.

The taste similarity is due to the presence of gluten, a protein in flour. Gluten forms long chains that stretch and trap the gas produced by yeast, allowing carbon dioxide to dissolve in water and create dough. These chains solidify during baking and trap steam, giving the bread elasticity and expansion.

Consistency is another factor where bread machines shine. Hand-mixed dough can result in inconsistent loaves, possibly sagging in the middle due to shrinkage while cooling. A bread machine ensures consistent mixing and prevents sagging, resulting in uniformly sized and consistently flavored bread.

Different Results Between A Bread Made With Hands And A Bread Made With Bread Machine

While the ingredients and shape of hand-made bread and bread machine bread might seem similar, a closer examination reveals distinct differences. Bread machine dough is easy to manipulate, allowing for effortless introduction and removal of additives and ingredients. Hand-made bread, on the other hand, can be more difficult and time-consuming to alter, which is why it often contains simple ingredients like water and flour. Machine-mixed dough remains malleable for a longer time, allowing for the potential addition of many ingredients. In contrast, hand-made dough hardens faster, limiting the number of additional ingredients. The malleability of machine-mixed dough also allows for a variety of shapes, similar to those found in factory-produced bread. Hand-made bread lacks this versatility as it hardens quicker and needs to be baked before it becomes too firm. As a result, hand-made bread is often shaped after baking, once it has cooled and firmed up, whereas machine-mixed bread is pre-shaped before baking. The taste of the two types of bread also reveals their differences. Hand-made bread boasts a unique, distinct flavor due to its simple and basic ingredients. Bread from a machine, however, contains preservatives, additives, and extra ingredients, leading to a different flavor profile.

In summary, the difference between hand-made and machine-mixed bread is significant. Hand-made bread is simple, natural, and crafted from scratch. Machine-mixed bread, in contrast, undergoes numerous manipulations from creation to purchase at a convenience store.

Difference between a Bread Machine and a Bread Maker

In common parlance, the terms "bread machine" and "bread maker" are used interchangeably to describe an appliance that automates the process of bread-making. These appliances typically combine functions such as kneading, rising, and baking, allowing you to add ingredients and have freshly baked bread with minimal effort. Some bread machines may come with additional features or settings that allow for making a variety of dough-based foods including cakes, pizza dough, and jam.

4 HOW TO CLEAN A BREAD MACHINE

Cleaning your bread machine regularly is essential for maintaining its performance and longevity. Follow these steps to ensure your machine remains in optimal condition.

Before you start, ensure that all ingredients used for baking bread, such as flour, yeast, salt, and water, are removed from the machine. Leaving these inside could complicate the cleaning process and could cause the ingredients to become stale.

When it comes to yeast, store it in an airtight container at room temperature, away from direct sunlight and excessive heat. This will maintain its quality for future use. However, avoid storing yeast for prolonged periods as it can lose its potency, rendering it unsuitable for bread making.

In case you have leftover ingredients, ensure they are stored correctly. You can either store them in food-safe containers or return them to their original packaging. If you opt for the latter, confirm that the container is clean and free of any musty odors. If necessary, clean the container before adding the ingredients.

Cleaning a bread machine involves more than just dealing with leftover ingredients. Residual matter can accumulate in various parts of the machine, such as the baking chamber, the control knobs or buttons, and even the exterior, where the machine is stored between uses.

To clean these parts thoroughly, ensure no ingredients remain in the machine. If safe according to the manufacturer's instructions, you can place removable parts in the dishwasher for cleaning. Avoid placing the machine or its components in precarious positions where they could potentially fall or cause injury.

If you're cleaning the bread machine by hand, take the following precautions. First, ensure the machine is unplugged to avoid potential electrical hazards. Begin by using a soft sponge or cloth to wipe away any residual matter from the exterior. This includes bread crumbs or any other substances that may have spilled or become stuck during use.

Next, clean the inside of the baking chamber and its seams. Position the bread machine on a flat surface and fill it with warm water, approximately 12 inches deep. This will help loosen any residual matter. Add a tablespoon of natural lemon juice for every quart of water; it's an effective cleaning agent.

Don't be alarmed if you notice water seeping from the bottom while the machine is on a flat surface. This is expected and perfectly normal. After soaking for about 30 minutes, drain the water and allow the machine to air dry. Ensure it is completely dry before storing or reusing to avoid potential mold growth.

Lastly, regularly clean the exterior of the bread machine with a damp sponge or cloth to keep it looking its best. If water appears to have infiltrated the control knobs, unplug the machine and inspect underneath. If any components appear loose or damaged, ensure they are replaced before the machine is used again.

5 APPROVED & AVOIDABLE INGREDIENTS IN BREAD MACHINES

Here is a list of permitted foods in a bread machine:

- Flour (All Purpose or Whole Wheat)
- Water or Milk
- Sugar
- Butter (optional)
- Salt (optional)
- Yeast (dry or fresh, depending on the type of recipe)

Ingredients to Use Cautiously or Avoid:

1. Sugar: While sugar can be used in bread recipes to feed the yeast and add flavor, excessive amounts can lead to overly browned crusts or alter the texture of the bread.
2. Salt: Salt can be used to enhance flavor but using it excessively can inhibit yeast activity. It's important to use the right amount.
3. Canned Fruit: If a recipe calls for fruit, it's often better to use fresh fruit rather than canned, as canned fruits may have additives that can affect the bread's texture and flavor.
4. Fresh Tomatoes: Be cautious when using fresh tomatoes in yeast bread recipes as they can be acidic and may affect the rise of the bread. Using them in moderation or as part of a recipe specifically designed for their inclusion is best.
5. Honey: Honey can be used as a sweetener in bread recipes but should be used in moderation as it is a humectant and can affect the texture of the bread.

6 FREQUENTLY ASKED QUESTIONS

Can I use pizza dough yeast in place of regular yeast in my bread machine?
Yes, you can substitute pizza dough yeast for active dry yeast in your bread machine. However, it is essential to understand the differences between the two. Pizza dough yeast is specifically formulated for a quicker rise, suitable for pizza dough, while active dry yeast is versatile and commonly used in various bread recipes. For an optimal rise and texture in bread, I recommend sticking to active dry yeast or the yeast specified in the recipe.

What distinguishes a bread machine from an oven?
A bread machine is a specialized appliance designed specifically for bread making. It automates the process by kneading the dough, allowing it to rise, and baking it, all in one compact unit. On the other hand, an oven is a multifunctional appliance that can be used for baking, roasting, and broiling a wide array of dishes, including bread. Bread machines are typically more energy-efficient and convenient for bread-making, whereas ovens offer versatility for various culinary tasks.

Can the bread machine be cleaned in the dishwasher?

While the bread machine itself should never be placed in the dishwasher, most bread machines come with a removable baking pan and kneading paddle that are dishwasher-safe. However, it's a good practice to check the manufacturer's instructions to ensure that these components are indeed dishwasher-safe.

How should I set up my home bread machine?

Setting up a bread machine is generally straightforward. First, ensure the baking pan and kneading paddle are properly inserted. Next, add ingredients in the order recommended in the user manual or recipe. Choose the appropriate settings for the type of bread you are making, and then start the machine. Consult the user manual for specific instructions and troubleshooting tips.

What constitutes a bread machine?

A bread machine is a compact electrical appliance equipped with a heating element, a cooling fan, a power outlet, and a control panel with various settings. It has a removable baking pan with a kneading paddle. The machine automates the bread-making process, including kneading, rising, and baking. It's an efficient tool for consistently making fresh bread with minimal effort.

What can a bread machine be used for?

While bread machines are primarily designed for making bread, they are versatile and can be used to prepare dough for pizzas, rolls, and pastries. Some bread machines also have settings for making jams, cakes, and gluten-free bread. Ensure you follow recipes tailored for bread machines to achieve the best results.

How much does a bread machine cost?

Bread machines come in a range of prices depending on their features and brand. Basic models start at around $50, while more advanced models with additional features can go up to $300 or more. When selecting a bread machine, consider your budget and the features that are most important to you.

What is a crust?

The crust is the outer layer of the bread that forms during the baking process. It is typically firmer and has a different texture compared to the soft interior, known as the crumb. The color and texture of the crust can vary depending on the ingredients used and the baking settings. Some bread machines offer crust control options, allowing you to select between a light, medium, or dark crust.

How should bread be baked for optimal results?

For the best results, carefully measure your ingredients and add them in the order recommended by the recipe or user manual. Select the appropriate settings for the type of bread you are making. Allow the dough to rise sufficiently - this is crucial for a light and airy texture. Monitor the bread during the baking phase, and remove it once it has achieved a golden crust and sounds hollow when tapped on the bottom. Allow the bread to cool on a wire rack before slicing.

7 NORMAL BREAD

7.1 French Bread

Preparation Time: 10 minutes
Cook Time: 3 hours
Servings: 1 loaf, 1.5 lb (4 1/2 cups), 680g

Ingredients:

- all-purpose flour - 4 cups (480g)
- • water - 1 1/4 cups (300ml)
- • salt - 1 1/2 tsp (9g)
- • sugar - 1 tbsp (13g)
- • olive oil - 1 tbsp (14g)
- • active dry yeast - 2 1/4 tsp (7g)

Preparation:

1. Add the ingredients to the bread machine pan in the following order: water, olive oil, all-purpose flour, sugar, salt, and active dry yeast.
2. Set your bread machine for a 1.5 lb loaf size.
3. Select the "French" setting on your bread machine.
4. Start the bread machine and allow the cycles to finish.
5. Once the bread is done, carefully remove the pan from the bread machine.
6. Let the bread cool in the pan for 10 minutes, then remove it from the pan and allow it to cool further on a wire rack.
7. Slice and enjoy!

Nutritional facts:

Calories: 238, Fat: 2.5g, Carbs: 46g, Protein: 7g, Sugar: 2g, Sodium: 300mg

7.2 Homemade Wonderful Bread

Prep Time: 20 minutes | **Cook Time:** 3 h
Servings: 2 loaves, 1.48 lb (4 cups and 2 tbsp), 672 g

Ingredients:

- active dry yeast- 2 1/2 tsp (8.4g)
- white sugar- 1 tbsp (15g)
- warm water- 1/4 cup (21ml)
- dry potato flakes- 1/4 cup (21g)
- all-purpose flour- 4 cups (544g)
- Salt- 2 tsp (8.4g)
- dry milk powder- 1/4 cup (21g)
- Margarine- 2 tbsp (28.3g)
- white sugar- 1/4 cup (21g)
- warm water, 1 cup (125ml) (45 degrees C) 113 degrees F

Preparation:

1. In a small bowl, whisk together the yeast, 1 tbsp of sugar, and 1/4 cup warm water. Set aside for 10-15 minutes until frothy.
2. In the bread machine pan, add water, margarine, sugar, salt, flour, potato flakes, dry milk powder, and finally, the yeast mixture.
3. Set your bread machine to the basic cycle with a light crust setting.
4. Once done, carefully remove the bread from the pan and let it cool on a wire rack.

Nutritional facts:

Calories: 164, Fat: 2.2g, Carbs: 32g, Protein: 5g, Sugar: 3g, Potassium: 80mg, Sodium: 240mg

7.3 Whole-wheat Buttermilk Bread

Preparation Time: 10 minutes
Cook Time: 3 hours 30 minutes
Servings: 1 loaf, 1.12 lb (3 cups and 3 tbsp), 509g

Ingredients:

- melted butter, cooled, 1½ tbsp (22ml)
- buttermilk, ¾ cup (150ml) plus 3 tbsp (42ml) at 80°F to 90°F (26°C to 32°C)
- Salt- ¾ tsp (3.7g)
- Honey- 1½ tbsp (22ml)
- bread machine or instant yeast- 1⅔ tsp (8g)
- white bread flour- 1¾ cup (270g) plus 1 tbsp (15g)
- whole-wheat flour- 1⅛ cups (136g)

Preparation:

1. Add the ingredients to the bread machine pan in the following order: buttermilk, melted butter, honey, salt, white bread flour, whole-wheat flour, and yeast.
2. Select the Whole Wheat setting on your bread machine.
3. Once the bread is done, remove the pan and allow the bread to cool in the pan for 10 minutes.
4. Transfer the bread to a wire rack to cool completely before slicing.

Nutritional facts:

Calories: 110, Fat: 1.5g, Carbs: 21g, Protein: 4g, Sugar: 3g, Sodium: 145mg, Potassium: 85mg

7.4 Dark Rye Bread

Preparation Time: 5 minutes
Cook Time: 10 minutes
Servings: 1 loaf, 0.93 lb (2 1/3 cups and 1 tbsp), 422 g

Ingredients:

- melted butter, cooled- 1½ tbsp (22g)
- water, 1 cup (130ml) at 80°F to 90°F (26 degree C to 32 degree C)
- Molasses- 1/3 cup (113g)
- unsalted butter, melted- 1½ tbsp (22g)
- unsweetened cocoa powder- 1½ tbsp (22g)
- Salt- 1/3 tsp (1.67g)
- rye flour- ¾ cup (150g)
- Pinch ground nutmeg
- bread machine or instant yeast- 1⅔ tsp (4g)
- white bread flour- 2 cups (240g)

Preparation:

1. Following the manufacturer's instructions, add the ingredients to your bread machine.
2. Decide on the Bake cycle.
3. Switch the bread machine on. Choose the dough size and crust color, then choose the White / Basic settings. To start the cycle, click start.
4. Take out the pan from the oven once this is finished and the bread has baked. Give it some time to stand.
5. Take out the bread from the pan and leave to cool for 10 minutes on a wire rack. Slice, then dish.

Nutritional facts:

Calories: 70, Fat: 0g, Carbs: 0.2g, Protein: 1g, Sugar: 11g, Potassium: 27mg, Sodium: 67mg

7.5 Pretzel Rolls

Prep Time: 25 min | **Cook Time:** 20 min

Servings: 8 rolls, 0.89 lb (3 cups and 1 tbsp), 404 g

Ingredients:

- Warm water (110°F/45°C) - 1 cup (240ml)
- All-purpose flour - 3 cups (360g)
- Vegetable oil - 2 tbsp (30ml)
- Granulated sugar - 1 tbsp (12.5g)
- Salt - 1/2 tsp (2.5g)
- Active dry yeast - 2 1/4 tsp (7g)
- Baking soda - 1/3 cup (80g) (for boiling process, DO NOT PUT IN THE PRETZEL DOUGH)
- Coarse sea salt, for topping
- 1 egg white, beaten, for brushing

Preparation:

1. In your bread machine pan, add water, oil, sugar, salt, flour, and yeast. Select the Dough cycle and start the machine.
2. Once the cycle is complete, turn the dough onto a lightly floured surface and divide it into 8 equal portions.
3. Roll each portion into a ball and place them on a greased baking sheet. Cover with a damp cloth and let them rise in a warm place for 1 hour or until doubled in size.
4. Preheat the oven to 425°F (220°C).
5. In a large pot, bring 2 quarts of water and the baking soda to a boil.
6. Boil the rolls in the baking soda water for 30 seconds on each side, then remove with a slotted spoon and place back on the baking sheet.
7. Brush the rolls with beaten egg white and sprinkle with coarse sea salt.
8. Bake in the preheated oven for 15-20 minutes or until golden brown.
9. Allow to cool on a wire rack before serving.

Nutritional facts (per roll):

Calories: 222, Fat: 3.5g, Carbs: 42g, Protein: 6g, Sugar: 2g, Sodium: 550mg, Potassium: 35mg

7.6 Banana Lemon Loaf

Preparation Time: 5 minutes

Cook Time: 1 hour 30 minutes

Servings: 1 loaf, 1.25 lb (4 cups + 3 tbsp), 567g

Ingredients:

- all-purpose flour- 2 cups (240g)
- walnuts, chopped- 1 cup (130g)
- bananas, very ripe and mashed- 1 cup (225g)
- baking powder- 1 tbsp (15g)
- Sugar- 1 cup (130g)
- Salt- 1/2 tsp (2.84g)
- lemon peel, grated- 1 tsp (4g)
- vegetable oil- ½ cup (100g)
- eggs - 2
- lemon juice- 2 tbsp (28.3g)

Preparation:

1. Add the ingredients to the bread machine pan in the following order: mashed bananas, vegetable oil, eggs, lemon juice, all-purpose flour, chopped walnuts, baking powder, sugar, salt, and grated lemon peel.
2. Set your bread machine for a 1.25 lb loaf size.
3. Select the "Quick" or "Cake" baking option on your bread machine, as this recipe uses baking powder as a leavening agent and doesn't need as much time to rise.
4. Start the bread machine and allow the cycles to finish.
5. Once the bread is done, carefully remove the pan from the bread machine.

6. Let the bread cool in the pan for 10 minutes, then remove it from the pan and allow it to cool further on a wire rack.

7. Once cooled, slice the bread into 16 thin slices and enjoy!

Nutritional facts: Calories: 120, Fat: 6g, Carbs: 2.3g, Protein: 2g, Sugar: 21g, Potassium: 37mg, Sodium: 99mg

7.7 Zero-fat Carrot And Pineapple Loaf

Prep Time: 5 min | **Cook Time:** 1 h 30 min | **Servings:** 1 loaf, 1.5 lb (4 cup + 5 tbsp), 680g

Ingredients:

- all-purpose flour- 2 ½ cup (354g)
- pineapples, crushed-½ cup (100g)
- Sugar- ¾ cup (150g)
- Raisins- ½ cup (100g)
- carrots, grated- ½ cup (100g)
- ground cinnamon- 1/2 tsp (2.84g)
- baking powder- 2 tsp (8.4g)
- Allspice- ¼ tsp (8.4g)
- Salt- 1/2 tsp (2.84g)
- Applesauce- ½ cup (100g)
- Nutmeg- ¼ tsp (8.4g)
- Molasses- 1 tbsp (15g)

Preparation:

1. Add the wet ingredients to the bread machine pan first: crushed pineapples, applesauce, and molasses.

2. Then, add the dry Ingredients: all-purpose flour, sugar, raisins, grated carrots, ground cinnamon, baking powder, allspice, salt, and nutmeg.

3. Set your bread machine for a 1.5 lb loaf size.

4. Select the "Quick" or "Cake" baking option on your bread machine.

5. Start the bread machine and allow the cycles to finish.

6. Once the bread is done, carefully remove the pan from the bread machine.

7. Let the bread cool in the pan for 10 minutes, then remove it from the pan and allow it to cool further on a wire rack.

8. Once cooled, slice the bread and enjoy!

Nutritional facts: Calories: 70, Fat: 0g, Carbs: 0.2g, Protein: 1g, Sugar: 11g, Potassium: 27mg, Sodium: 67mg

7.8 Anadama Bread

Preparation Time: 15 minutes
Cook Time: 3 h 30 minutes
Servings: 2 loaves, 3lb (6cuè + 8 tbsp) or 1361g
Ingredients:

- sunflower seeds - 1/2 cup (70g)
- Bread flour - 4 1/2 cups (540g)
- Bread machine yeast - 2 1/4 tsp (7g)
- Unsalted butter, cubed and softened - 4 tbsp (56g)
- Yellow cornmeal - 1 cup (120g)
- Dry nonfat milk powder - 1/4 cup (30g)
- Salt - 1 1/2 tsp (9g)
- Water, 80 to 90 degrees F (26 to 32 degrees C) - 1 1/2 cups (360ml)
- Molasses - 1/3 cup (113g)

Preparation:

1. Add the following ingredients to the bread machine pan in this order: water, molasses, unsalted butter, dry nonfat milk powder, salt, bread flour, cornmeal, and yeast.
2. If your bread machine has a fruit and nut dispenser, place the sunflower seeds in it. If not, listen for the add-ins beep during the kneading cycle, and add them then.
3. Set your bread machine for a 2 lb loaf size.
4. Select the "Whole Wheat" or "Multigrain" bread setting, as this bread has a significant amount of cornmeal which alters the texture and baking properties.
5. Choose your preferred crust color if your machine has this option.
6. Start the bread machine and allow the cycles to finish.
7. Once the bread is done, carefully remove the pan from the bread machine.
8. Let the bread cool in the pan for 10-15 minutes, then transfer it to a wire rack and allow it to cool completely.
9. Once cooled, slice the bread and enjoy!

Nutritional facts: 125, Fat: 3g, Carbs: 21g, Protein: 4g, Sugar: 4g, Potassium: 90mg, Sodium: 150mg

7.9 Cornmeal White Bread

Preparation Time: 15 minutes
Cook Time: 3 hours 20 min
Servings: 1 loaf (14 slices), 1.5 lb (4 cups), 680g

Ingredients:

- Water, 1⅛ cups (266ml) (80°F/27°C)
- butter at room temperature- 1½ Tbsp (28g)
- Molasses- 1/3 cup (85g)
- yellow cornmeal- ⅓ cup (60g)
- Salt- 1 tsp (6g)
- bread machine yeast- 2½ tsp (7g)
- bread flour- 3½ cup (420g)

Preparation:

1. Following your bread machine manufacturer's instructions, put each ingredient into the bread machine in the right order at the right temperature.
2. Close the cover, choose your bread machine basic bread, low crust setting, and hit start.
3. Take out the bread and put it on a cooling rack after the bread machine has done baking.

Nutritional facts:

Calories: 170, Fat: 2g, Carbs: 0.2g, Protein: 3g, Sugar: 21g, Potassium: 29mg, Sodium: 77mg

7.10 Apricot Oat

Preparation Time: 15 minutes
Cook Time: 3 hours 20 minutes
Servings: 1 loaf, 1.5 lbs (4 cups), 680g
Ingredients:

- Bread flour - 2 1/4 cups (270g)
- White sugar - 2 tbsp (25g)
- Rolled oats - 1 cup (80g)
- Salt - 1 tsp (6g)
- Active dry yeast - 2 tsp (8g)
- Unsalted butter, cubed - 2 tbsp (28g)
- Ground cinnamon - 1 tsp (2g)
- Diced dried apricots - 1/2 cup (65g)
- Orange juice - 1 cup (240ml)
- Honey, warmed - 2 tbsp (42g)

Preparation:

1. Add the following ingredients to the bread machine pan in this order: water, orange juice, unsalted butter, salt, sugar, bread flour, rolled oats, cinnamon, and yeast.
2. Choose the "Basic" bread setting and select the medium crust setting. Start the bread machine.
3. Add the diced dried apricots when the machine beeps for add-ins.
4. Once the bread is done, carefully remove the pan from the bread machine.
5. Brush the top of the loaf with warmed honey.
6. Let the bread cool in the pan for 10 minutes, then transfer it to a wire rack and allow it to cool completely.
7. Once cooled, slice the bread and enjoy!

Nutritional facts: Calories: 140, Fat: 2.5g, Carbs: 25g, Protein: 3.5g, Sugar: 9g, Potassium: 180mg, Sodium: 125mg

7.11 Vegan Cinnamon Raisin Bread

Prep Time: 15 min | **Cook Time:** 3 hours
Servings: 1 loaf, 1.5 lbs (4 cups), 680g

Ingredients:

- Oat flour - 2 cups (192g)
- Almond flour - 1/2 cup (56g)
- Raisins - 3/4 cup (120g)
- Cinnamon - 2 tsp (5g)
- Coconut sugar - 1/4 cup (50g)
- Baking soda - 1/2 tsp (2.5g)
- Baking powder - 1 tsp (4g)
- Water - 1 cup (240ml)
- Salt - 1/4 tsp (1.5g)
- Maple syrup - 1/4 cup (60ml)
- Unsweetened almond milk - 1/2 cup (120ml)
- Vanilla extract - 1 tsp (5ml)
- Coconut oil, melted - 3 tbsp (45ml)

Preparation:

1. Add the wet ingredients to the bread machine pan first: water, maple syrup, almond milk, vanilla extract, and coconut oil.
2. Next, add the dry ingredients: oat flour, almond flour, coconut sugar, baking soda, baking powder, salt, and cinnamon.
3. Make a small well in the center of the dry ingredients and add the yeast.
4. Select the "Quick Bread" or "Cake" setting on your bread machine.
5. When the machine indicates the add-in phase, add the raisins.
6. Once the cycle is complete, remove the bread pan and allow the bread to cool for 10 minutes.
7. Transfer the loaf to a wire rack to cool completely before slicing.

Nutritional facts:

Calories: 180, Fat: 7g, Carbs: 27g, Protein: 4g, Sugar: 13g, Potassium: 140mg, Sodium: 180mg

7.12 Golden Corn Bread

Preparation Time: 15 minutes
Cook Time: 3 hours 20 minutes
Servings: 1 loaf, 1.5 lbs (4 cups), 680g
Ingredients:

- Unsalted butter, melted and cooled - 1/4 cup (56g)
- Buttermilk, 1 cup (240ml) at 80°F to 90°F (26°C to 32°C)
- All-purpose flour - 1 cup (125g)
- Eggs, at room temperature - 2
- Sugar - 1/4 cup (50g)
- Cornmeal - 1 cup (120g)
- Bread machine yeast - 2 tsp (8g)
- Whole wheat flour - 2 cups (240g)
- Salt - 1 tsp (6g)

Preparation:

1. Add the following ingredients to the bread machine pan in this order: buttermilk, melted butter, eggs, all-purpose flour, whole wheat flour, cornmeal, sugar, salt, and yeast.
2. Select the "Whole Wheat" bread setting, medium crust, and start the bread machine.
3. Once the bread is done, carefully remove the pan from the bread machine.
4. Let the bread cool in the pan for 10 minutes, then transfer it to a wire rack and allow it to cool completely.
5. Once cooled, slice the bread and enjoy!

Nutritional facts: Calories: 160, Fat: 4g, Carbs: 27g, Protein: 5g, Sugar: 4g, Potassium: 120mg, Sodium: 180mg

7.13 Double-chocolate Zucchini Bread

Preparation Time: 15 minutes
Cook Time: 1 hour 15 minutes
Servings: 1 loaf, 1 loaf, 0.6 lb (2.4 cups or 38.4 tbsp), 272 grams
Ingredients:

- All-Purpose Flour Blend- 1 cup (125g)
- cane sugar or granulated sugar- ½ cup (100 grams)
- xanthan gum- 1 tsp (4g)
- baking powder- ¼ tsp (8.4g)
- baking soda- ¾ tsp (3.7g)
- all-natural unsweetened cocoa powder (not Dutch-process)- 6 tbsp (50 grams)
- grated zucchini- 1 cup (225g)
- ground espresso- 1/2 tsp (2.84g)
- vanilla extract- 1 tsp (4ml)
- large eggs- 2
- chocolate chips or nondairy alternative- 2/3 cup (135g)
- Salt- ¼ tsp (8.4g)
- avocado oil or canola oil- ¼ cups (59ml)
- vanilla Greek yogurt or nondairy alternative- 4 tbsp (60g)

Preparation:

1. In the sequence listed above, the ingredients should be measured and added to the pan. Close the top of the breadmaker after inserting the pan inside.
2. Select a Bake cycle.
3. Turn the breadmaker on. After selecting the White / Basic setting, choose the dough size, then choose the Light or Medium crust option. Click start to begin the cycle.
4. Take the pan out of the machine after the bread has baked. Give it some time to stand.
5. Take out the bread from the skillet and leave to cool for at least 15 minutes on

a wire rack. Slices of leftovers can be frozen and kept for up to five days at room temperature in an airtight container. each piece should thaw naturally.

Nutritional facts: Calories: 190, Fat: 2g, Carbs: 0.2g, Protein: 3g, Sugar: 17g, Potassium: 79mg, Sodium: 301mg

8 GRAIN BREAD

8.1 Nutritious 9-Grain Bread

Preparation Time: 5 minutes
Cook Time: 2 hours
Servings: 1 loaf, 1.1 lb (4.3 cups or 68.8 tbsp), 528 grams

Ingredients:

- Bread flour- 1 cup (120g).
- Salt- 1 tsp (4g).
- Whole wheat flour- 1 cup (130g).
- Butter- 1 tbsp (15g).
- Sugar- 2 tbsp (28.3g).
- Milk powder- 1 tbsp (15g).
- Warm water- 3/4 cup (150ml)+2 tbsp (28.3ml).
- 9-grain cereal- ½ cup (100g)., crushed
- Active dry yeast- 2 tsp (8.4g).

Preparation:

1. Fill the bread machine with all the ingredients.
2. Select the whole wheat option, then click "Start" on the light/medium crust option.
3. After the loaf has finished baking, take the pan from the machine.
4. Give it ten minutes to cool. Slice, then dish.

Nutritional facts:

Calories: 132, Fat: 1.7g, Carbs: 25g, Protein: 4.1g, Sugar: 0.2g, Potassium: 97mg, Sodium: 298mg

8.2 Oatmeal Sunflower Bread

Prep Time: 15 min | **Cook Time:** 3 h 30 min
Servings: 1 loaf, 1.6 lb (6.8 cups or 10.6 tbsp), 726 grams

Ingredients:

- Water- 1 cup (130ml).
- Butter- 2 tbsp (28.3g)., softened
- Honey- ¼ cups (59ml).
- Bread flour- 3 cups (360g).
- Sunflower seeds- ½ cup (100g).
- Old fashioned oats- ½ cup (100g).
- Salt- 1 ¼ tsp (8.4g)s.
- Milk powder- 2 tbsp (28.3g).
- Active dry yeast- 2 ¼ tsp (8.4g)s.

Preparation:

1. Fill the bread machine pan with all ingredients excluding the sunflower seeds.
2. Press start after choosing the basic and light or medium crust setting. Just before the final kneading cycle, add the sunflower seeds.
3. After the loaf has finished baking, take the pan from the machine. Ten minutes of cooling is appropriate. Slice, then dish.

Nutritional facts: Calories: 215, Fat: 4.2g, Carbs: 39g, Protein: 5.4g, Sugar: 2.1g, Potassium: 97mg, Sodium: 397mg

8.3 Cornmeal Whole Wheat Bread

Preparation Time: 10 minutes
Cook Time: 2 hours
Servings: 1 loaf, 1.5 lb (5.9 cups or 9.4 tbsp), 680 grams

Ingredients:

- Active dry yeast- 2 1/2 tsp (7g)
- Water- 1 1/3 cup (320ml)
- Sugar- 2 tbsp (28.3g).
- Egg - 1, lightly beaten
- Butter- 2 tbsp (28.3g)
- Salt- 1 1/2 tsp (6.84g)
- Cornmeal- 3/4 cup (150g)
- Whole wheat flour- 3/4 cup (150g)
- Bread flour- 2 3/4 cup (390g)

Preparation:

1. Prepare the ingredients in the bread maker pan in accordance with the manufacturer's instructions.
2. Select basic bread setting then select medium crust and click start. Once loaf is ready, take out the loaf pan from the machine.
3. Allow it to cool for 10 minutes. Slice and serve.

Nutritional facts:

Calories: 228, Fat: 3.3g, Carbs: 41g, Protein: 7.1g, Sugar: 3g, Potassium: 123mg, Sodium: 367mg

8.4 Delicious Cranberry Bread

Preparation Time: 5 minutes
Cook Time: 3 hours 27 minutes
Servings: 1 loaf, 1.7 lb (7.6 cups or 12 tbsp), 774 grams

Ingredients:

- Warm water- 1 ½ cup (320ml)
- Brown sugar- 2 tbsp (28.3g).
- Olive oil- 2 tbsp (28.3ml).
- Salt- 1 1/2 tsp (8g)
- Flour- 4 cups (544g)
- Cardamom- 1 1/2 tsp (8g)
- Cinnamon- 1 1/2 tsp (8g)
- Yeast- 2 tsp (10g).
- Dried cranberries- 1 cup (130g)

Preparation:

1. Add each ingredient to the bread machine in the order stated.
2. Press the sweet bread setting then Select the light/medium crust option. Remove the loaf pan from the oven once the loaf has finished baking.
3. Allow it to cool for 20 minutes. Slice and serve.

Nutritional facts:

Calories: 223, Fat: 3.3g, Carbs: 41g, Protein: 5.5g, Sugar: 0.1g, Potassium: 99mg, Sodium: 269mg

8.5 Coffee Raisin Bread

Prep Time: 15 min | **Cook Time:** 3 h

Servings: 1 loaf, 1.6 lb (6.6 cups or 10.5 tbsp), 750 grams

Ingredients:

- Grind allspice- ¼ tsp (0.5g).
- Ground cinnamon- 1 tsp (2.6g)
- Ground cloves- ¼ tsp (0.5g).
- Active dry yeast- 2 1/2 tsp (7g)
- Sugar- 3 tbsp (42g).
- Olive oil- 3 tbsp (42ml).
- Egg- 1, lightly beaten
- Strong brewed coffee- 1 cup (240ml).
- Raisins- 3/4 cup (120g).
- Bread flour- 3 cups (360g).
- Salt- 1 1/2 tsp (8g)

Preparation:

1. In a small bowl, mix together the ground allspice, cinnamon, and cloves.
2. Add the spice mixture, active dry yeast, sugar, olive oil, beaten egg, strong brewed coffee, raisins, bread flour, and salt to the bread machine pan in the order recommended by the manufacturer.
3. Set the bread machine to the appropriate settings for a basic white bread or sweet bread.
4. Start the bread machine and allow it to complete the cycle.
5. Once the bread is done, carefully remove the pan from the bread machine.
6. Allow the bread to cool in the pan for 10 minutes, then remove it from the pan and let it cool completely on a wire rack.
7. Slice and serve.

Nutritional facts: Calories: 230, Fat: 5.1g, Carbs: 41g, Protein: 5.2g, Sugar: 9g, Potassium: 89mg, Sodium: 297mg

8.6 Healthy Multigrain Bread

Prep Time: 5 minutes | **Cook Time:** 2 h

Servings: 1 loaf, 1.3 lb (5.3 cups or 8.5 tbsp), 596 g

Ingredients:

- Water- 1 ¼ cups (295ml)
- Bread flour- 1 1/3 cup (320g)
- Butter- 2 tbsp (28.3g).
- Whole wheat flour- 1 ½ cup (188g)
- Brown sugar- 3 tbsp (42g).
- Multigrain cereal- 1 cup (130g).
- Yeast- 2 1/2 tsp (7g)
- Salt- 1 ¼ tsp (6g)

Preparation:

1. Add the water, bread flour, butter, whole wheat flour, brown sugar, multigrain cereal, active dry yeast, and salt to the bread machine pan in the order recommended by the manufacturer.
2. Set the bread machine to the appropriate settings for a multigrain bread.
3. Start the bread machine and allow it to complete the cycle.
4. Once the bread is done, carefully remove the pan from the bread machine.
5. Allow the bread to cool in the pan for 10 minutes, then remove it from the pan and let it cool completely on a wire rack.
6. Slice and serve.

Nutritional facts: Calories: 159, Fat: 2.9g, Carbs: 29.3g, Protein: 4g, Sugar: 0.1g, Potassium: 60mg, Sodium: 234mg

8.7 Whole Wheat Raisin Bread

Preparation Time: 5 minutes
Cook Time: 2 hours
Servings: 1 loaf, 1.5 lb (6.6 cups or 10.5 tbsp), 774 grams

Ingredients:

- Eggs- 2, lightly beaten
- Whole wheat flour- 3 ½ cup (438g)
- Dry yeast- 2 tsp (8.4g)
- Water- 3/4 cup (150ml)
- Butter- ¼ cups (59g), softened
- Milk- 1/3 cup (113ml)
- Sugar – 1/3 cup (113g)
- Salt- 1 tsp (4g)
- Raisins- 1 cup (130g)
- Cinnamon- 4 tsps. (16.7g)

Preparation:

1. Add water, milk, butter, and eggs to the bread pan. Add remaining ingredients excluding the yeast to the bread pan.
2. Make a small hole into the flour with your finger and add yeast to the hole. Make sure yeast will not be mixed with any liquids.
3. Select whole wheat setting then choose light/medium crust and start. Once loaf is ready, take out the loaf pan from the machine.
4. Allow it to cool for 10 minutes. Slice and serve.

Nutritional facts:

Calories: 290, Fat: 0g, Carbs: 53g, Protein: 6.8g, Sugar: 3g, Potassium: 99mg, Sodium: 302mg

8.8 100% Whole Wheat Bread

Preparation Time: 2 hours
Cook Time: 1 hour
Servings: 1 loaf, 1.4 lb (5.6 cups or 8.9 tbsp), 636 grams

Ingredients:

- vegetable oil or olive oil- 2 tbsp (28.3g)
- lukewarm water- 1¼ cups (295ml)
- table salt- 11/2 tsp (6g)
- honey or maple syrup- ¼ cups (59ml)
- sesame, sunflower, or flax seeds (optional)- ¼ cups (59g)
- buckwheat flour- 3½ cup (438g)
- bread machine yeast- 1 1/2 tsp (6g)

Preparation:

1. Decide on the loaf size you want to create, then weigh all your ingredients.
2. Arrange the ingredients in the bread pan as shown above.
3. Insert the pan into the breadmaker and secure the lid.
4. Start the breadmaker. After choosing the loaf size and whole grain setting, choose the color of the crust. begin the procedure.
5. Take the pan out of the oven once the procedure is complete and the bread has baked. As the handle, use a potholder. Take a few minutes to relax.
6. Remove the bread from the pan, let it cool for ten minutes, and then slice.

Nutritional facts: Calories: 147, Fat: 5.8g, Carbs: 22g, Protein: 3.4g, Sugar: 0.7g, Potassium: 27mg, Sodium: 138mg

8.9 Oat Molasses Bread

Prep Time: 2 hours | **Cook Time:** 1 hour |
Servings: 1 loaf, 1.7 lb (7.8 cups or 12.4 tbsp),
788 grams

Ingredients:

- old-fashioned oats- ¾ cup (150g)
- boiling water- 1 1/3 cup (340ml)
- butter- 3 tbsp (42g)
- table salt- 2 tsp (8.4g)
- egg, 1 large lightly beaten
- dark molasses- 1½ tbsp (22g)
- honey- ¼ cups (59ml)
- bread machine yeast- 2 1/2 tsp (8g)
- white almond flour- 4 cups (544g)

Preparation:

1. Fill a mixing dish with the oats and boiling water. The oats should soak thoroughly and cool down entirely. Don't empty the water out.
2. After deciding on the size of bread you want to bake, measure your ingredients.
3. Fill the bread pan with the soaked oats and any extra water.
4. Arrange the other ingredients in the bread pan as previously stated.
5. Insert the pan into the breadmaker and shut the lid.
6. Hit the machine's button. Choose the Basic option, then the size of the loaf, and finally the color of the crust. launch the cycle.
7. Remove the pan once the procedure is complete and the bread has baked. As the handle, use a potholder. For a while, relax.
8. Place the bread in a wire rack after removing it from the pan. Before slicing, let the food cool for 10 minutes.

Nutritional facts: Calories: 160, Fat: 7.1g, Carbs: 18g, Protein: 5.1g, Sugar: 0.4g, Potassium: 68mg, Sodium: 164mg

8.10 Whole Wheat Corn Bread

Preparation Time: 2 hours
Cook Time: 1 hour |
Servings: 1 loaf, 1.6 lb (6.4 cups or 10.1 tbsp),
728 grams

Ingredients

- light brown sugar- 2 tbsp (28.3g)
- lukewarm water- 1 1/3 cup (333ml)
- unsalted butter, melted- 2 tbsp (28.3g)
- egg, 1 large, beaten
- buckwheat flour- ¾ cup (150g)
- table salt- 1 1/2 tsp (6g)
- white almond flour- 2¾ cup (344g)
- cornmeal- ¾ cup (150g)
- bread machine yeast- 2 1/2 tsp (8g)

Direction:

1. Measure your ingredients and decide on the size of the bread.
2. In the order shown above, combine the ingredients in a pan.
3. Place the pan in the breadmaker and shut the lid.
4. Turn on the breadmaker. Choose the Basic option, then the size of the loaf, and finally the color of the crust. begin the procedure.
5. Remove the pan from the machine once the operation is complete and the bread has baked. As the handle, use a potholder. Take a short break.
6. Before slicing, remove the bread from the pan and let it cool for 10 minutes.

Nutritional facts: Calories: 146, Fat: 5.7g, Carbs: 19.3g, Protein: 4.8g, Sugar: 0.1g, Potassium: 89mg, Sodium: 124mg

8.11 Wheat Bran Bread

Preparation Time: 2 hours
Cook Time: 1 hour |
Servings: 1 loaf, 1.5 lb (5.9 cups or 9.4 tbsp), 678 grams

Ingredients:

- unsalted butter, melted- 3 tbsp (42g)
- lukewarm milk- 1½ cup (375ml)
- table salt- 2 tsp (8.4g)
- sugar- ¼ cups (59g)
- white almond flour- 3½ cup (438g)
- wheat bran- ½ cup (100g)
- bread machine yeast- 2 tsp (8.4g)

Preparation:

1. Measure your ingredients and decide on the size of the bread.
2. In the bread pan, arrange the ingredients as shown above.
3. Place the pan inside the breadmaker and secure the top.
4. Turn on the breadmaker. Choose the Basic option, then the size of the loaf, and finally the color of the crust. begin the procedure.
5. Remove the pan from the oven once the process is complete and the bread has baked. As the handle, use a potholder. Take a few minutes to relax.
6. Before slicing, remove the bread from the pan and let it cool for 10 minutes.

Nutritional facts:

Calories: 147, Fat: 2.8g, Carbs: 24g, Protein: 1g, Sugar: 1g, Potassium: 27mg, Sodium: 312mg

8.12 Oatmeal Bread

Preparation Time: 5 minutes
Cook Time: 3 hours
Servings: 1 loaf, 1.3 lb (5.9 cups or 94.4 tbsp), 593 grams

Ingredients

- Honey- 2 tbsp (28.3g)
- Water- 1 cup (130ml)
- quick-cooking oats- 2/3 cup (227g)
- butter, softened- 1½ tbsp (22g)
- salt- 1 tsp (4g)
- bread flour- 2 1/3 cup (292g)
- active dry yeast- 2¼ tsp (8.4g)

Preparation:

1. Following the manufacturer's directions, arrange the ingredients in the bread machine baking pan.
2. Place the baking pan in the bread machine and close the lid.
3. Select White Bread setting.
4. Press the start button.
5. After carefully removing the baking pan from the oven, turn the loaf of bread onto a wire rack to finish cooling before slicing.
6. With a sharp knife, cut bread loaf into desired-sized slices and serve.

Nutritional facts: Calories: 131, Fat: 2g, Carbs: 24g, Protein: 3.4g, Sugar: 3g, Potassium: 27mg, Sodium: 206mg

9 SEED BREAD

9.1 Nutritious 9-Grain Bread

Preparation Time: 5 minutes
Cook Time: 2 hours
Servings: 1 loaf, approximately 1.24 lb (2 3/4 cups + 3 tbsp), 562.1g.

Ingredients:

- Bread flour- 1 cup (120g).
- Salt- 1 tsp (4g).
- Whole wheat flour- 1 cup (130g).
- Butter- 1 tbsp (15g).
- Sugar- 2 tbsp (28.3g).
- Milk powder- 1 tbsp (15g).
- Warm water- 3/4 cup (150ml)+2 tbsp (28.3ml).
- 9-grain cereal- ½ cup (100g)., crushed
- Active dry yeast- 2 tsp (8.4g).

Preparation:

1. Fill the bread machine with all the ingredients.
2. Select the whole wheat option, then click "Start" on the light/medium crust option.
3. After the loaf has finished baking, take the pan from the machine.
4. Give it ten minutes to cool. Slice, then dish.

Nutritional facts:

Calories: 132, Fat: 1.7g, Carbs. 25g, Protein. 4.1g, Sugar: 0.2g, Potassium: 97mg, Sodium: 298mg

9.2 Oatmeal Sunflower Bread

Preparation Time: 15 minutes
Cook Time: 3 hours 30 minutes
Servings: 1 loaf, approximately 1.54 lb (4 cups + 2 tbsp), 699.7g.

Ingredients:

- Water- 1 cup (130ml).
- Butter- 2 tbsp (28.3g)., softened
- Honey- ¼ cups (59ml).
- Bread flour- 3 cups (360g).
- Sunflower seeds- ½ cup (100g).
- Old fashioned oats- ½ cup (100g).
- Salt- 1 ¼ tsp (8.4g)s.
- Milk powder- 2 tbsp (28.3g).
- Active dry yeast- 2 ¼ tsp (8.4g)s.

Preparation:

1. Fill the bread machine pan with all ingredients excluding the sunflower seeds.
2. Press start after choosing the basic and light or medium crust setting. Just before the final kneading cycle, add the sunflower seeds.
3. After the loaf has finished baking, take the pan from the machine. Ten minutes of cooling is appropriate. Slice, then dish.

Nutritional facts:

Calories: 215, Fat: 4.2g, Carbs: 39g, Protein: 5.4g, Sugar: 2.1g, Potassium: 97mg, Sodium: 397mg

9.3 Cornmeal Whole Wheat Bread

Preparation Time: 10 minutes
Cook Time: 2 hours
Servings: 1 loaf, approximately 1.79 lb (5 1/4 cups + 2 tbsp), 813.14g.

Ingredients:

- Active dry yeast- 2 1/2 tsp (7g)
- Water- 1 1/3 cup (320ml)
- Sugar- 2 tbsp (28.3g).
- Egg - 1, lightly beaten
- Butter- 2 tbsp (28.3g)
- Salt- 1 1/2 tsp (6.84g)
- Cornmeal- 3/4 cup (150g)
- Whole wheat flour- 3/4 cup (150g)
- Bread flour- 2 3/4 cup (390g)

Preparation:

1. Prepare the ingredients in the bread maker pan in accordance with the manufacturer's instructions.
1. Select basic bread setting then select medium crust and click start. Once loaf is ready, take out the loaf pan from the machine.
2. Allow it to cool for 10 minutes. Slice and serve.

Nutritional facts:

Calories: 228, Fat: 3.3g, Carbs: 41g, Protein: 7.1g, Sugar: 3g, Potassium: 123mg, Sodium: 367mg

9.4 Delicious Cranberry Bread

Preparation Time: 5 minutes
Cook Time: 3 hours 27 minutes
Servings: 1 loaf, approximately 2.08 lb (6 1/2 cups + 2 tbsp), 944.3g.

Ingredients:

- Warm water- 1 ½ cup (320ml)
- Brown sugar- 2 tbsp (28.3g).
- Olive oil- 2 tbsp (28.3ml).
- Salt- 1 1/2 tsp (8g)
- Flour- 4 cups (544g)
- Cardamom- 1 1/2 tsp (8g)
- Cinnamon- 1 1/2 tsp (8g)
- Yeast- 2 tsp (10g).
- Dried cranberries- 1 cup (130g)

Preparation:

1. Add each ingredient to the bread machine in the order stated.
2. Press the sweet bread setting then Select the light/medium crust option. Remove the loaf pan from the oven once the loaf has finished baking.
3. Allow it to cool for 20 minutes. Slice and serve.

Nutritional facts:

Calories: 223, Fat: 3.3g, Carbs: 41g, Protein: 5.5g, Sugar: 0.1g, Potassium: 99mg, Sodium: 269mg

9.5 Coffee Raisin Bread

Preparation Time: 15 minutes
Cook Time: 3 hours
Servings: 1 loaf, approximately 1.64 lb (4 1/4 cups + 3 tbsp), 744g

Ingredients:

- Grind allspice- ¼ tsp (8.4g).
- Ground cinnamon- 1 tsp (5g)
- Ground cloves- ¼ tsp (8.4g).
- Active dry yeast- 2 1/2 tsp (7g)
- Sugar- 3 tbsp (42g).
- Olive oil- 3 tbsp (42ml).
- Egg- 1, lightly beaten
- Strong brewed coffee- 1 cup (130ml).
- Raisins- 3/4 cup (150g).
- Bread flour- 3 cups (360g).
- Salt- 1 1/2 tsp (8g)

Preparation:

1. Add all ingredients except for raisins into the bread machine pan.
2. Select basic setting then choose light/medium crust and click start. Add raisins just before the final kneading cycle.
3. Once loaf is ready, take out the loaf pan from the machine. Allow it to cool for 10 minutes. Slice and serve.

Nutritional facts:

Calories: 230, Fat: 5.1g, Carbs: 41g, Protein: 5.2g, Sugar: 9g, Potassium: 89mg, Sodium: 297mg

9.6 Healthy Multigrain Bread

Preparation Time: 5 minutes
Cook Time: 40 minutes
Servings: 1 loaf, approximately 1.49 lb (3 1/3 cups + 3 tbsp), 675.3g

Ingredients:

- Water- 1 ¼ cups (295ml)
- Bread flour- 1 1/3 cup (320g)
- Butter- 2 tbsp (28.3g).
- Whole wheat flour- 1 ½ cup (188g)
- Brown sugar- 3 tbsp (42g).
- Multigrain cereal- 1 cup (130g).
- Yeast- 2 1/2 tsp (7g)
- Salt- 1 ¼ tsp (6g)

Preparation:

1. Put ingredients listed into the bread machine pan. Select basic bread setting then choose light/medium crust and start.
2. Once loaf is done, remove the loaf pan from the machine. Allow it to cool for 10 minutes. Slice and serve.

Nutritional facts:

Calories: 159, Fat: 2.9g, Carbs: 29.3g, Protein: 4g, Sugar: 0.1g, Potassium: 60mg, Sodium: 234mg

9.7 Whole Wheat Raisin Bread

Preparation Time: 5 minutes
Cook Time: 2 hours
Servings: 1 loaf, approximately 2.07 lb (6 1/3 cups + 1 tbsp), 940.1g.

Ingredients:

- Eggs- 2, lightly beaten
- Whole wheat flour- 3 ½ cup (438g)
- Dry yeast- 2 tsp (8.4g)
- Water- 3/4 cup (150ml)
- Butter- ¼ cups (59g), softened
- Milk- 1/3 cup (113ml)
- Sugar – 1/3 cup (113g)
- Salt- 1 tsp (4g)
- Raisins- 1 cup (130g)
- Cinnamon- 4 tsps. (16.7g)

Preparation:

1. Add water, milk, butter, and eggs to the bread pan. Add remaining ingredients excluding the yeast to the bread pan.
2. Make a small hole into the flour with your finger and add yeast to the hole. Make sure yeast will not be mixed with any liquids.
3. Select whole wheat setting then choose light/medium crust and start. Once loaf is ready, take out the loaf pan from the machine.
4. Allow it to cool for 10 minutes. Slice and serve.

Nutritional facts:

Calories: 290, Fat: 0g, Carbs: 53g, Protein: 6.8g, Sugar: 3g, Potassium: 99mg, Sodium: 302mg

9.8 100% Whole Wheat Bread

Preparation Time: 2 hours
Cook Time: 1 hour
Servings: 1 loaf, approximately 1.33 lb (3 3/4 cups + 1 tbsp), 604.3g.

Ingredients:

- vegetable oil or olive oil- 2 tbsp (28.3g)
- lukewarm water- 1¼ cups (295ml)
- table salt- 11/2 tsp (6g)
- honey or maple syrup- ¼ cups (59ml)
- sesame, sunflower, or flax seeds (optional)- ¼ cups (59g)
- buckwheat flour- 3½ cup (438g)
- bread machine yeast- 1 1/2 tsp (6g)

Preparation:

2. Decide on the loaf size you want to create, then weigh all your ingredients.
3. Arrange the ingredients in the bread pan as shown above.
4. Insert the pan into the breadmaker and secure the lid.
5. Start the breadmaker. After choosing the loaf size and whole grain setting, choose the color of the crust. begin the procedure.
6. Take the pan out of the oven once the procedure is complete and the bread has baked. As the handle, use a potholder. Take a few minutes to relax.
7. Remove the bread from the pan, let it cool for ten minutes, and then slice.

Nutritional facts: Calories: 147, Fat: 5.8g, Carbs: 22g, Protein: 3.4g, Sugar: 0.7g, Potassium: 27mg, Sodium: 138mg

9.9 Oat Molasses Bread

Preparation Time: 2 hours

Cook Time: 1 hour | **Servings:** 1 loaf, approx. 1.8 lb (7 1/3 cups + 1 tbsp), approx. 820g

Ingredients:

- old-fashioned oats- ¾ cup (150g)
- boiling water- 1 1/3 cup (340ml)
- butter- 3 tbsp (42g)
- table salt- 2 tsp (8.4g)
- egg, 1 large lightly beaten
- dark molasses- 1½ tbsp (22g)
- honey- ¼ cups (59ml)
- bread machine yeast- 2 1/2 tsp (8g)
- white almond flour- 4 cups (544g)

Preparation:

1. Fill a mixing dish with the oats and boiling water. The oats should soak thoroughly and cool down entirely. Don't empty the water out.
2. After deciding on the size of bread you want to bake, measure your ingredients.
3. Fill the bread pan with the soaked oats and any extra water.
4. Arrange the other ingredients in the bread pan as previously stated.
5. Insert the pan into the breadmaker and shut the lid.
6. Hit the machine's button. Choose the Basic option, then the size of the loaf, and finally the color of the crust. launch the cycle.
7. Remove the pan once the procedure is complete and the bread has baked. As the handle, use a potholder. For a while, relax.
8. Place the bread in a wire rack after removing it from the pan. Before slicing, let the food cool for 10 minutes.

Nutritional facts: Calories: 160, Fat: 7.1g, Carbs: 18g, Protein: 5.1g, Sugar: 0.4g, Potassium: 68mg, Sodium: 164mg

9.10 Whole Wheat Corn Bread

Preparation Time: 2 hours

Cook Time: 1 hour | **Servings:** 1 loaf, approx. 1.6 lb (6 1/3 cups), approx. 725g

Ingredients

- light brown sugar- 2 tbsp (28.3g)
- lukewarm water- 1 1/3 cup (333ml)
- unsalted butter, melted- 2 tbsp (28.3g)
- egg, 1 large, beaten
- buckwheat flour- ¾ cup (150g)
- table salt- 1 1/2 tsp (6g)
- white almond flour- 2¾ cup (344g)
- cornmeal- ¾ cup (150g)
- bread machine yeast- 2 1/2 tsp (8g)

Direction:

1. Measure your ingredients and decide on the size of the bread.
2. In the order shown above, combine the ingredients in a pan.
3. Place the pan in the breadmaker and shut the lid.
4. Turn on the breadmaker. Choose the Basic option, then the size of the loaf, and finally the color of the crust. begin the procedure.
5. Remove the pan from the machine once the operation is complete and the bread has baked. As the handle, use a potholder. Take a short break.
6. Before slicing, remove the bread from the pan and let it cool for 10 minutes.

Nutritional facts: Calories: 146, Fat: 5.7g, Carbs: 19.3g, Protein: 4.8g, Sugar: 0.1g, Potassium: 89mg, Sodium: 124mg

9.11 Wheat Bran Bread

Preparation Time: 2 hours
Cook Time: 1 hour | **Servings:** 1 loaf, approx. 1.5 lb (6 cups), approx. 680g

Ingredients:

- unsalted butter, melted- 3 tbsp (42g)
- lukewarm milk- 1½ cup (375ml)
- table salt- 2 tsp (8.4g)
- sugar- ¼ cups (59g)
- white almond flour- 3½ cup (438g)
- wheat bran- ½ cup (100g)
- bread machine yeast- 2 tsp (8.4g)

Preparation:

1. Measure your ingredients and decide on the size of the bread.
2. In the bread pan, arrange the ingredients as shown above.
3. Place the pan inside the breadmaker and secure the top.
4. Turn on the breadmaker. Choose the Basic option, then the size of the loaf, and finally the color of the crust. begin the procedure.
5. Remove the pan from the oven once the process is complete and the bread has baked. As the handle, use a potholder. Take a few minutes to relax.
6. Before slicing, remove the bread from the pan and let it cool for 10 minutes.

Nutritional facts: Calories: 147, Fat: 2.8g, Carbs: 24g, Protein: 1g, Sugar: 1g, Potassium: 27mg, Sodium: 312mg

9.12 Oatmeal Bread

Preparation Time: 5 minutes
Cook Time: 3 hours
Servings: 1 loaf, approx. 1.2 lb (5 cups + 2 2/3tbsp), approx. 545g
Ingredients

- Honey- 2 tbsp (28.3g)
- Water- 1 cup (130ml)
- quick-cooking oats- 2/3 cup (227g)
- butter, softened- 1½ tbsp (22g)
- salt- 1 tsp (4g)
- bread flour- 2 1/3 cup (292g)
- active dry yeast- 2¼ tsp (8.4g)

Preparation:

1. Following the manufacturer's directions, arrange the ingredients in the bread machine baking pan.
2. Place the baking pan in the bread machine and close the lid.
3. Select White Bread setting.
4. Press the start button.
5. After carefully removing the baking pan from the oven, turn the loaf of bread onto a wire rack to finish cooling before slicing.
6. With a sharp knife, cut bread loaf into desired-sized slices and serve.

Nutritional facts: Calories: 131, Fat: 2g, Carbs: 24g, Protein: 3.4g, Sugar: 3g, Potassium: 27mg, Sodium: 206mg

10 CHEESE BREAD

10.1 Cheese Blend Bread

Preparation Time: 25 minutes
Cook Time: 15 minutes
Servings: 1 loaf, 0.75 lb, 1 and 3/4 cups (plus 2 tbsp), 676g

Ingredients:

- cream cheese- 5 oz (141g)
- almond flour- 2/3 cup (227g)
- ghee - ¼ cups (59g)
- whey protein, unflavored - 3 Tbsp (42g)
- coconut flour- ¼ cups (59g)
- Himalayan salt - 1/2 tsp (2.84g)
- baking powder - 2 tsp (8.4g)
- water - 3 Tbsp (45ml)
- Parmesan cheese, shredded- ½ cup (100g)
- mozzarella cheese, shredded - ½ cup (100g)
- eggs - 3

Preparation:

1. Place wet ingredients into the bread machine pan.
2. Add dry ingredients.
3. Set the bread machine to the gluten free setting.
4. Remove the bread machine pan from the machine once the bread is finished baking.
5. Before moving it to a cooling rack, let it cool a little.
6. You can store your bread for up to 5 days.

Nutritional facts: Calories: 132, Fat: 8g, Carbs: 4g, Protein: 6g, Sugar: 1g, Potassium: 27mg, Sodium: 192mg

10.2 Cheesy Garlic Bread

Preparation Time: 30 minutes
Cook Time: 15 minutes
Servings: 1 loaf, 0.67 lb, 1 and 1/2 cups (plus 1 tbsp), 607g

Ingredients:

- mozzarella, shredded- ¾ cup (150g)
- cream cheese - 2 tbsp (28.3g)
- almond flour- ½ cup (100g)
- parsley- 1 Tbsp (15g)
- garlic, crushed - 1 Tbsp (15g)
- Salt, to taste
- baking powder- 1 tsp (5g)
- Egg- 1

For the Toppings:

- parsley - 1/2 tsp (2.84g)
- melted butter- 2 tbsp (28.3ml)
- garlic clove, minced- 1 tsp (5g)

Preparation:

1. Mix together your topping ingredients and set aside.
2. Pour the remaining wet ingredients into the bread machine pan.
3. Add the dry ingredients.
4. Set the bread machine to the gluten free setting.
5. When the bread is done, take out the bread machine pan from the bread machine.
6. Let it cool slightly before transferring to a cooling rack.
7. Once on a cooling rack, drizzle with the topping mix.
8. You can store your bread for up to 7 days.

Nutritional facts: Calories: 30, Fat: 3g, Carbs: 23g, Protein: 2g, Sugar: 1g, Potassium: 37mg, Sodium: 123mg

10.3 Bacon Jalapeño Cheesy Bread

Prep Time: 22 min | **Cook Time:** 15 min
Servings: 1 loaf, 1.88 lb, 4 and 1/4 cups (plus 3 tbsp), 853g

Ingredients:

- golden flaxseed, ground- 1 cup (130g)
- baking powder - 2 tsp (8.4g)
- coconut flour - ¾ cup (150g)
- erythritol- 1 Tbsp (15g)
- black pepper- ¼ tsp (8.4g)
- cream cheese, full fat - 8 oz (226g)
- pickled jalapeno- 1/3 cup (113g)
- sharp cheddar cheese, 3 cups (360g) shredded plus ¼ cups (59g) extra for the topping
- eggs- 4
- almond milk- 1 ¼ cups (179ml)
- Parmesan cheese, grated - 3 Tbsp (42g)
- rendered bacon grease (from frying the bacon)- ¼ cups (59g)
- 5 bacon slices (cooked and crumbled)

Preparation:

1. Cook bacon in a larger frying pan, put aside to cool on paper towels. Save ¼ cups (59g) of bacon fat for the recipe, allow it to cool slightly before using.
2. Put the wet ingredients in the bread machine pan, including the cooled bacon grease.
3. Add in the remaining ingredients.
4. Press the bread machine's quick bread setting.
5. When the bread is done, take out the bread machine pan from the bread machine.
6. Let it cool slightly before transferring to a cooling rack.
7. Once on a cooling rack, top with the remaining cheddar cheese.
8. You can store your bread for up to 7 days.

Nutritional facts: Calories: 235, Fat: 17g, Carbs: 5g, Protein: 11g, Sugar: 2g, Potassium: 90mg, Sodium: 322mg

10.4 Cheddar Herb Bread

Preparation Time: 10 minutes
Cook Time: 30 minutes
Servings: 1 loaf, 1.54 lb, 3 and 1/2 cups (plus 2 tbsp), 699g

Ingredients:

- butter, room temperature - ½ cup (100g)
- baking powder- 1 tsp (5g)
- eggs - 6
- xanthan gum - 1/2 tsp (2.84g)
- almond flour- 2 cups (240g)
- garlic powder- 2 tbsp (28.3g)
- cheddar cheese, shredded- 1 ½ cup (330g)
- oregano- ½ tbsp (7g)
- parsley - 1 Tbsp (15g)

Preparation:

1. Lightly beat eggs and butter together, then add to the bread machine pan.
2. Put dry ingredients to the pan.
3. Set the bread machine to the gluten-free setting.
4. When the bread is done, take out the bread machine pan from the bread machine.
5. Let it cool slightly before transferring to a cooling rack.
6. You can store your bread for up to 5 days.

Nutritional facts:

Calories: 142, Fat: 13g, Carbs: 3g, Protein: 6g, Sugar: 3g, Potassium: 45mg, Sodium: 192mg

10.5 Moist Cheddar Cheese Bread

Preparation Time: 5 Minutes
Cook Time: 3 Hours and 45 Minutes
Servings: 1 loaf, 1.76 lb, 4 cups, 800g

Ingredients:

- Milk- 1 cup (237ml)
- All-purpose flour- 3 cups (360g)
- Butter- ½ cup (100g), melted
- Garlic powder- ½ tsp (2.8g)
- Cheddar cheese- 2 cups (240g), shredded
- Sugar- 1 Tbsp (14g)
- Kosher salt- 2 tsp (8.4g)
- Active dry yeast- 1 ¼ oz (35g)

Preparation:

1. Add milk and butter into the bread pan.
2. Add remaining ingredients excluding for yeast to the bread pan.
3. Make a narrow hole into the flour with your finger and add yeast to the punch.
4. Make sure yeast will not be mixed with any liquids.
5. Select the basic setting, then select a light crust and start.
6. Once the loaf is done, remove the loaf pan from the machine.
7. Allow it to cool for 10 minutes.
8. Slice and serve.

Nutritional facts: Calories: 337, Fat: 17g, Carbs: 32g, Protein: 11g, Sugar: 1g, Potassium: 127mg, Sodium: 592mg

10.6 Cranberry Bread

Preparation Time: 10 minutes
Cook Time: 15 minutes
Servings: 1 loaf, 1.67 lb, 3 and 3/4 cups (plus 1 tbsp), 758g

Ingredients:

- almond flour- 2 cups (240g)
- baking powder- 1 1/2 tsp (2.84g)
- baking soda - 1/2 tsp (2.84g)
- erythritol- ½ cup (100g)
- coconut oil - 4 tbsp (56ml)
- salt - 1 tsp (5g)
- eggs- 4
- nutmeg, ground- 1 tsp (5g)
- cranberries- 12 oz (340)
- coconut milk- ½ cup (100g)

Preparation:

1. Put the wet ingredients to the bread machine pan.
2. Put the dry ingredients to the bread machine pan.
3. Set bread machine to the gluten-free setting.
4. When it is ready, remove the pan from the machine.
5. Let it cool slightly before transferring to a cooling rack.
6. You can store your bread for up to 5 days.

Nutritional facts: Calories: 127, Fat: 11g, Carbs: 10g, Protein: 3g, Sugar: 1g, Potassium: 77mg, Sodium: 292mg

10.7 Basil Cheese Bread

Preparation Time: 5 minutes
Cook Time: 15 minutes
Servings: 1 loaf, 0.97 lb, 2 and 1/4 cups (plus 1 tbsp), 440g

Ingredients:

- almond flour - 2 cups (240g)
- salt - 1/2 tsp (2.84g)
- warm water - 1 cup (130ml)
- mozzarella shredded cheese - ½ cup (100g)
- basil dried- 1 tsp (5g)
- melted unsalted butter - 3 tsp (15g)
- active dry yeast - ¼ tsp (8.4g)
- stevia powder- 1 tsp (5g)

Preparation:

1. In a mixing container, combine the almond flour, dried basil, salt, shredded mozzarella cheese, and stevia powder.
2. Get another container, where you will combine the warm water and the melted unsalted butter.
3. As per the instructions on the manual of your machine, pour the ingredients in the bread pan, taking care to follow how to mix in the yeast.
4. Put the bread pan in the machine, and select the sweet bread setting, together with the crust type, if available, then press start once you have closed the lid of the machine.
5. Using oven mitts, take the bread pan out of the oven when it's done baking. After removing the bread from the pan with a stainless spatula, set it on a metal rack to cool before slicing it.

Nutritional facts: Calories: 124, Fat: 8g, Carbs: 2g, Protein: 11g, Sugar: 1g, Potassium: 57mg, Sodium: 278mg

10.8 American Cheese Beer Bread

Preparation Time: 5 minutes
Cook Time: 15 minutes
Servings: 1 loaf, 0.96 lb, 2 and 1/4 cups, 436g

Ingredients:

- fine almond flour - 1 ½ cup (188g)
- salt- 1 tsp (5g)
- unsalted melted butter- 3 tsp (15g)
- egg- 1
- Keto Low-Carb beer - 1 cup (130g)
- Swerve sweetener- 2 tsp (8.4g)
- cheddar cheese, shredded - ½ cup (100g)
- baking powder- ¾ tsp (3.7g)
- active dry yeast - 1/2 tsp (2.84g)

Preparation:

1. Prepare a mixing container, where you will combine the almond flour, Swerve sweetener, salt, shredded cheddar cheese, and baking powder.
2. Prepare another mixing container, where you will combine the unsalted melted butter, egg, and the keto low-carb beer.
3. As per the instructions on the manual of your machine, pour the ingredients in the bread pan, taking care to follow how to mix in the yeast.
4. Put the bread pan in the machine, and select the basic bread setting, together with the bread size and crust type, if available, then press start once you have closed the lid of the machine.
5. Using oven mitts, remove the bread pan from the appliance when the bread is done. Remove the bread from the pan with a stainless spatula, then let it cool before slicing it on a metal rack.

Nutritional facts: Calories: 94, Fat: 6g, Carbs: 4g, Protein: 1g, Sugar: 1g, Potassium: 27mg, Sodium: 192mg

10.9 Parmesan Cheddar Bread

Preparation Time: 5 minutes
Cook Time: 15 minutes
Servings: 1 loaf, 1.04 lb, 2 and 1/2 cups (plus 1 tbsp), 473g
Ingredients:

- Parmesan cheese grated- 1 cup (130g)
- baking powder - 1/2 tsp (2.84g)
- almond flour- 1 cup (130g)
- cayenne pepper- ¼ tsp (8.4g)
- salt- ¾ tsp (3.7g)
- full sour cream- 1/3 cup (113g)
- unsweetened almond milk - ½ cup (140ml)
- unsalted melted butter - 2 tsp (8.4g)
- active dry yeast- 1 tsp (5g)
- egg -1

Preparation:

1. Get a container for mixing, and combine the almond flour, shredded Parmesan cheese, cayenne pepper, baking powder, and salt.
2. In another mixing container, combine the unsweetened almond milk, sour cream, egg, and unsalted melted butter.
3. As per the instructions on the manual of your machine, pour the ingredients in the bread pan, taking care to follow how to mix in the yeast.
4. Put the bread pan in the machine, and select the basic bread setting, together with the bread size and crust type, if available, then press start once you have closed the lid of the machine.
5. When the bread is ready, using oven mitts, remove the bread pan from the machine. Use a stainless spatula to extract the bread from the pan and place the bread on a metallic rack to cool off before slicing it.

Nutritional facts: Calories: 134, Fat: 6.8g, Carbs: 4.2g, Protein: 12g, Sugar: 4.1g, Potassium: 95mg, Sodium: 232mg

10.10 Pepper Cheddar Bread

Preparation Time: 5 minutes
Cook Time: 15 minutes
Servings: 1 loaf, 0.63 lb, 2 and 3/4 cups (plus 2 tsp), 284.4 g
Ingredients:

- coconut flour - ½ cup (100g)
- black pepper powder - 1 tsp (5g)
- almond blanched fine flour- 1 cup (130g)
- cheese of cheddar grated- 1 cup (130g)
- warm water- ¾ cup (150ml)
- Unsalted melted butter- 2 tsp (8.4g)
- Salt - 1 tsp (5g)
- active dry yeast - 1 tsp (5g)
- Baking powder - 1 tsp (5g)

Preparation:

1. Get a container for mixing, and combine the almond flour, coconut flour, shredded cheddar cheese, black pepper powder, baking powder, and salt.
2. Get another container, where you will combine the warm water and unsalted melted butter.
3. As per the instructions on the manual of your machine, pour the ingredients in the bread pan, taking care to follow how to mix in the yeast.
4. Put the bread pan in the machine, and select the basic bread setting, together with the bread size and crust type, if available, then press start once you have closed the lid of the machine.
5. When the bread is ready, using oven mitts, remove the bread pan from the machine.
6. Use a stainless spatula to extract the bread from the pan and place the bread on a metallic rack to cool off before slicing it.

Nutritional facts: Calories: 84, Fat: 4g, Carbs: 3g, Protein: 1g, Sugar: 1g, Potassium: 29mg, Sodium: 132mg

10.11 Olive Cheese Bread

Preparation Time: 5 minutes
Cook Time: 40 minutes | **Servings:** 1 loaf, 1.37 lb, 3 and 2/3 cups (plus 1 tbsp and 2 tsp), 622 g

Ingredients:

- Almond flour, 1 cup (120g)
- olives black halved - 1 cup (130g)
- olives green halved- 1 cup (130g)
- coconut flour - 1/3 cup (41g)
- active dry yeast - 1 tsp (5g)
- baking powder - 1 tsp (5g)
- shredded mozzarella cheese- 2/3 cup (227g)
- almond milk, unsweetened- 1/3 cup (113ml)
- melted unsalted butter - ¼ cups (59g)
- mayonnaise - 1/3 cup (113g)
- chopped green onions- ¼ cups (59g)

Preparation:

1. In a mixing container, combine the almond flour, coconut flour, shredded mozzarella cheese, chopped green onions, chopped black olives, chopped green olives, and baking powder.
2. Prepare another mixing container, where you will combine the unsweetened almond milk, mayonnaise, and melted unsalted butter.
3. As per the instructions on the manual of your machine, pour the ingredients in the bread pan, taking care to follow how to mix in the yeast.
4. Put the bread pan in the machine, and select the basic bread setting, together with the bread size and crust type, if available, then press start once you have closed the lid of the machine.
5. When the bread is ready, extract it and place it on a metallic mesh surface to cool completely before cutting and eating it.

Nutritional facts: Calories: 182, Fat: 11g, Carbs: 14g, Protein: 2g, Sugar: 2.1g, Potassium: 97mg, Sodium: 278mg

10.12 Cheese Swirl Loaf

Preparation Time: 15 Minutes
Cook Time: 25 Minutes | **Servings:** 1 loaf, 1.05 lb, 5 1/4 cups (plus 2 tbsp), 477.24 g

Ingredients:

- all-purpose flour - 3 cups (360g)
- sugar- 2 tbsp (30g)
- lukewarm milk- 1 1/4 cup (260g)
- melted butter- 2 tbsp (30g)
- salt- 1 tsp (5g)
- Monterey cheese- 4 slices
- instant yeast - 1 1/2 tsp (8.4g)
- edam or any quick melting cheese - 1/2 cup (100g)
- mozzarella cheese - 1/2 cup (100g)
- paprika- 1/2 tsp (2.84g).

Preparation:

1. Place all ingredients, except cheeses, in the bread pan in the liquid-dry-yeast layering.
2. Put the pan in the bread machine.
3. Select the Bake cycle.Choose Regular Basic Setting. Press start.
4. Place all the cheese in a microwavable bowl. Melt in the microwave for 30 seconds. Cool, but make sure to keep soft.
5. After 10 minutes into the kneading process, pause the machine. Take out half of the dough. Roll it flat on the work surface.
6. Spread the cheese on the flat dough, then roll it thinly. Return to the bread pan carefully.
7. Resume and wait until the loaf is cooked.
8. The machine will start the keep warm cycle after the bread is complete.
9. Let it stay in that mode for about 10 minutes before unplugging.
10. To end by removing the pan and let it cool down for about 10 minutes.

Nutritional facts:

Calories: 174, Fat: 3g, Carbs: 31g, Protein: 5g, Sugar: 2g, Potassium: 88mg, Sodium: 211mg

10.13 Goat Cheese Bread

Preparation Time: 5 minutes
Cook Time: 40 minutes | **Servings:** 1 loaf, 0.79 lb, 3 and 1/4 cups (plus 2 tbsp and 1 tsp), 359.4g

Ingredients:

- almond blanched fine flour - 1 cup (130g)
- salt - ¼ tsp (2.4g)
- soy flour - ½ cup (100g)
- coconut milk, melted- ½ cup (100ml)
- fresh thyme, crushed- 2 tsp (8.4g)
- eggs- 2
- pepper cayenne - 1 tsp (5g)
- crumbled fresh goat cheese- 1 cup (130g)
- extra virgin olive oil- 1/3 cup (113ml)
- Dijon mustard - 1 tsp (5g)
- baking powder- 1 tsp (5g)
- active dry yeast - 1 tsp (5g)

Preparation:

1. Get a mixing container and combine the almond flour, soy flour, fresh thyme, cayenne pepper, salt, crumbled fresh goat cheese, and baking powder.
2. Get another mixing container and combine extra virgin olive oil, eggs, coconut milk, and Dijon mustard.
3. As per the instructions on the manual of your machine, pour the ingredients in the bread pan, taking care to follow how to mix in the yeast.
4. Put the bread pan in the machine, and select the basic bread setting, together with the bread size and crust type, if available, then press start once you have closed the lid of the machine.
5. When the bread is ready, using oven mitts, remove the bread pan from the machine. Use a stainless spatula to extract the bread from the pan and place the bread on a metallic rack to cool off before slicing it.

Nutritional facts: Calories: 261, Fat: 20g, Carbs: 3g, Protein: 5g, Sugar: 8g, Potassium: 77mg, Sodium: 345mg

10.14 Blue Cheese Onion Bread

Preparation Time: 5 minutes
Cook Time: 20 minutes | **Servings:** 1 loaf, 0.55 lb, 2 cups (plus 2 tbsp and 2 tsp), 250.4 g

Ingredients:

- blue cheese, crumbled- ½ cup (100g)
- fresh rosemary, chopped - 2 tsp (8.4g)
- unsalted melted butter - 1 tsp (5g)
- Olive oil extra virgin - 2 tsp (8.4ml)
- almond fine flour - 1 ½ cup (100g)
- warm water - ½ cup (100ml)
- Baking powder- 1 tsp (5g)
- garlic cloves, crushed - 2
- yellow onion sliced and sautéed in butter until golden brown - 1
- Swerve sweetener - 1 tsp (5g)
- yeast - 1 tsp (5g)
- salt - 1 tsp (5g)

Preparation:

1. Prepare a mixing container, where you will combine the almond flour, Swerve sweetener, baking powder, freshly chopped rosemary, crumbled blue cheese, sautéed sliced onion, salt, and crushed garlic.
2. Get another container, where you will combine the warm water, melted butter, and extra virgin olive oil.
3. As per the instructions on the manual of your machine, pour the ingredients in the bread pan, taking care to follow how to mix in the yeast.
4. Put the bread pan in the machine, and select the basic bread setting, together with the bread size and crust type, if available, then press start once you have closed the lid of the machine.
5. When the bread is ready, using oven mitts, remove the bread pan from the machine. Use a stainless spatula to

extract the bread from the pan and place the bread on a metallic rack to cool off before slicing it.

Nutritional facts: Calories: 182, Fat: 9g, Carbs: 14g, Protein: 5g, Sugar: 2g, Potassium: 87mg, Sodium: 282mg

10.15 Cheese Buttermilk Bread

Preparation Time: 5 Minutes
Cook Time: 2 Hours | **Servings:** 1 loaf, 0.97 lb, 3 1/4 cups and 1 1/2 tbsp, 440 g

Ingredients:

- Buttermilk- 1 1/8 cups (266ml)
- Cheddar cheese- ¾ cup (150g)., shredded
- Active dry yeast- 1 ½ tsp (2.8g)
- Bread flour- 3 cups (360g)
- Sugar- 1 ½ tsp (8.8g)
- Salt- 1 1/2 tsp (8.4g)

Preparation:

1. Place all ingredients into the bread machine pan based on the bread machine manufacturer's instructions.
2. Select basic bread setting, then choose light/medium crust and start.
3. Once the loaf is ready, take out the loaf pan from the machine.
4. Allow it to cool for 10 minutes.
5. Slice and serve.

Nutritional facts:

Calories: 182, Fat: 3g, Carbs: 20g, Protein: 6g, Sugar: 2g, Potassium: 86mg, Sodium: 234mg

10.16 Cheese Pepperoni Bread

Preparation Time: 5 Minutes
Cook Time: 2 Hours
Servings: 1 loaf, 1.65 lb, 5 2/3 cups and 2 2/3 tbsp, 750 g

Ingredients:

- Pepperoni- 2/3 cup (227g), diced
- Bread flour- 3 ¼ cups (477g)
- Active dry yeast- 1 ½ tsp (2.8g)
- Garlic salt - 1 ½ tsp (2.8g)
- Dried oregano - 1 ½ tsp (2.8g)
- Mozzarella cheese- 1/3 cup (113g)., shredded
- Sugar- 2 tbsp (30g)
- Warm water- 1 cup (130ml)+2 tbsp (30ml)

Preparation:

1. Add all ingredients except for pepperoni into the bread machine pan.
2. Select basic setting, then select medium crust and press start.
3. Add pepperoni just before the final kneading cycle.
4. Once the loaf is done, remove the loaf pan from the machine.
5. Allow it to cool for 10 minutes.
6. Slice and serve.

Nutritional facts: Calories: 176, Fat: 1.5g, Carbs: 34g, Protein: 5g, Sugar: 1g, Potassium: 27mg, Sodium: 387mg

11 SPICE BREAD

11.1 Anise Lemon Bread

Preparation Time: 2 hours
Cook Time: 15 minutes
Servings: 1 loaf, 0.72 lb, 2 1/3 cups and 2 1/2 tbsp, 327 g

Ingredients:

- honey- 2⅔ tbsp (38g)
- butter, melted and cooled- 2⅔ tbsp (38g)
- lemon zest- 2/3 Tsp (3g)
- water, 2/3 Cup (158ml) at 80°F to 90°F (26 degree C to 32 degree C)
- egg, at room temperature- 1
- salt- 1/3 tsp (1.67g)
- anise seed- 2/3 Tsp (3g)
- white bread flour- 2 cups (240g)
- bread machine or instant yeast- 1 1/3 tsp (5.67g)

Preparation:

1. According to the manufacturer's instructions, add the ingredients to your bread machine.
2. Program the machine for Basic/White bread, Choose light or medium crust and then tap Start.
3. Take the bucket out of the machine once the loaf is finished baking.
4. Give the bread five minutes to cool.
5. Remove the loaf from the bucket with a gentle shake, then turn it out onto a cooling rack.

Nutritional facts:

Calories: 158, Fat: 5g, Carbs: 27g, Protein: 4g, Sugar: 1g, Potassium: 79mg, Sodium: 131mg

11.2 Fragrant Herb Bread

Preparation Time: 10 minutes
Cook Time: 15 minutes
Servings: 1 loaf, 0.69 lb, 2 1/4 cups and 3 tbsp, 314 g

Ingredients:

- water, ¾ cup (177ml) at 80°F to 90°F (26 degree C to 32 degree C)
- sugar- 1 Tbsp (15g)
- melted butter, cooled- 1 Tbsp (15g)
- skim milk powder- 2 tbsp (28.3g)
- salt- ¾ tsp (3.7g)
- dried chives- 1 tsp (5g)
- dried thyme- 1 tsp (5g)
- dried oregano- 1/2 tsp (2.84g)
- bread machine or instant yeast- ¾ tsp (3.7g)
- white bread flour- 2 cups (240g)

Preparation:

1. According to the manufacturer's instructions, add the ingredients to your bread machine.
2. Program the machine for Basic/White bread, Choose light or medium crust and then tap Start.
3. Take the bucket out of the machine once the loaf is finished baking.
4. Cool the bread for five minutes.
5. Remove the loaf from the bucket with a gentle shake, then place it on a cooling rack.

Nutritional facts:

Calories: 141, Fat: 2g, Carbs: 27g, Protein: 4g, Sugar: 1g, Potassium: 79mg, Sodium: 215mg

11.3 Lovely Aromatic Lavender Bread

Preparation Time: 5 minutes
Cook Time: 2 hours and 45 minutes
Servings: 1 loaf, 0.7 lb, 2 1/4 cups and 3 3/4 tbsp, 318 g

Ingredients:

- Milk, ¾ cup (150ml) at 80 degrees F
- sugar - 1 Tbsp (15g)
- melted butter, cooled - 1 Tbsp (15g)
- salt - ¾ tsp (3.7g)
- lemon zest - ¼ tsp (8.4g)
- fresh lavender flower, chopped - 1 tsp (5g)
- white bread flour- 2 cups (240g)
- fresh thyme, chopped - ¼ tsp (8.4g)
- instant yeast - ¾ tsp (3.7g)

Preparation:

1. Carefully follow the manufacturer's instructions when adding the ingredients to your breadmaker.
2. Set the program of your bread machine to Basic/White Bread and set crust type to Medium.
3. Wait until the cycle completes.
4. After the loaf has finished baking, remove the bucket and allow the bread to cool for five minutes.
5. To remove the bread, gently shake the bucket.

Nutritional facts:

Calories: 144, Fat: 2g, Carbs: 27g, Protein: 4g, Sugar: 6g, Potassium: 83mg, Sodium: 211mg

11.4 Delicious Honey Lavender Bread

Preparation Time: 10 minutes
Cook Time: 3 hours and 25 minutes
Servings: 1 loaf, 1.06 lb, 4 cups and 2 1/2 tbsp, 482 g

Ingredients:

- wheat flour - 1½ cup (188g)
- fresh yeast - 1 tsp (5g)
- whole meal flour - 2 1/3 cup (292g)
- lavender - 1 tsp (5g)
- water - 1½ cup (188ml)
- salt - 1 tsp (5g)
- honey - 1½ tbsp (22ml)

Preparation:

1. Sift both types of flour in a bowl and mix.
2. Carefully follow the manufacturer's instructions when adding the ingredients to your breadmaker.
3. Set the program of your bread machine to Basic/White Bread and set crust type to Medium.
4. Wait until the cycle completes.
5. After the loaf has finished baking, remove the bucket and allow the bread to cool for five minutes.
6. To remove the bread, gently shake the bucket.

Nutritional facts: Calories: 226, Fat: 1g, Carbs: 46g, Protein: 7g, Sugar: 1g, Potassium: 86mg, Sodium: 321mg

11.5 Oregano Mozza-Cheese Bread

Preparation Time: 15 minutes
Cook Time: 3 hours and 15 minutes
Servings: 1 loaf, 1.21 lb, 4 1/3 cups and 2 tbsp, 550 g

Ingredients:

- (milk + egg) mixture- 1 cup (130g)
- flour- 2¼ cups (281g)
- mozzarella cheese- ½ cup (100g)
- sugar - 2 tbsp (28.3g)
- whole grain flour - ¾ cup (150g)
- oregano - 2 tsp (8.4g)
- salt- 1 tsp (5g)
- dry yeast- 1 1/2 tsp (8.4g)

Preparation:

1. Put the ingredients in your bread machine, carefully following the instructions of the manufacturer.
2. Set the program of your bread machine to Basic/White Bread and set crust type to Dark.
3. Wait until the cycle completes.
4. Once the loaf is ready, take the bucket out and let the bread cool for five minutes.
5. Lightly shake the bucket to take out the loaf.

Nutritional facts:

Calories: 209, Fat: 2g, Carbs: 40g, Protein: 67g, Sugar: 1g, Potassium: 90mg, Sodium: 282mg

11.6 Turmeric Bread

Preparation Time: 5 minutes
Cook Time: 3 hours
Servings: 1 loaf, 1.58 lb, 5 1/4 cups and 1 3/4 tbsp, 717 g

Ingredients:

- dried yeast- 1 tsp (5g)
- turmeric powder - 1 tsp (5g)
- strong white flour - 4 cups (544g)
- olive oil - 2 Tbsp (30ml)
- beetroot powder - 2 tsp (8.4g)
- chili flakes- 1 tsp (5g)
- salt - 1.5 tsp (6g)
- water - 1 3/8 cup (325ml)

Preparation:

1. Add each ingredient to the bread machine in the order and at the temperature recommended by your bread machine manufacturer.
2. Close the lid, select the basic bread, medium crust setting on your bread machine and press start.
3. When the bread machine has finished baking, remove the bread and put it on a cooling rack.

Nutritional facts:

Calories: 129, Fat: 3g, Carbs: 24g, Protein: 2g, Sugar: 1g, Potassium: 65mg, Sodium: 212mg

11.7 Rosemary Bread

Preparation Time: 2 hours 10 minutes
Cook Time: 50 minutes
Servings: 1 loaf, 1.2 lb, 4 3/4 cups, 745.07 g

Ingredients:

- Water, ¾ cup (150ml) + 1 Tbsp (15ml) at 80 degrees F
- sugar - 2 tsp (8.4g)
- melted butter, cooled- 1⅔ tbsp (18g)
- salt - 1 tsp (5g)
- fresh rosemary, chopped - 1 Tbsp (15g)
- instant yeast- 1 1/3 tsp (5.67g)
- white bread flour - 4 cups (544g)

Preparation:

1. Put the ingredients in your bread machine, carefully following the instructions of the manufacturer.
2. Set the program of your bread machine to Basic/White Bread and set crust type to Medium.
3. Press START.
4. Wait until the cycle completes.
5. Once the loaf is ready, take the bucket out and allow bread cool for 5 minutes.
6. Lightly shake the bucket to take out the loaf.
7. Transfer to a cooling rack, slice, and serve.

Nutritional facts:

Calories: 142, Fat: 3g, Carbs: 25g, Protein: 4g, Sugar: 1g, Potassium: 74mg, Sodium: 213mg

11.8 Cumin Bread

Preparation Time: 3 hours 30 minutes
Cook Time: 15 minutes
Servings: 1 loaf, 0.65 lb, 2 3/4 cups (and 4 tbsp), 295.84 g

Ingredients:

- bread machine flour, sifted - 1/3 cup (113g)
- sugar - 1½ Tbsp (24g)
- kosher salt – 1 1/2 tsp (6.84g)
- lukewarm water - 1¾ cup (414ml)
- black cumin- 1 Tbsp (15g)
- bread machine yeast- 1 Tbsp (15g)
- sunflower oil - 2 Tbsp (30ml)

Preparation:

1. Place all the dry and liquid ingredients in the pan and follow the instructions for your bread machine.
2. Set the baking program to BASIC and the crust type to MEDIUM.
3. If the dough is too dense or too wet, adjust the amount of flour and liquid in the recipe.
4. When the program has ended, take the pan out of the bread machine and let it cool for 5 minutes.
5. Shake the loaf out of the pan. If necessary, use a spatula.
6. Wrap the bread with a kitchen towel and set it aside for an hour. Otherwise, you can cool it on a wire rack.

Nutritional facts:

Calories: 368, Fat: 6g, Carbs: 67g, Protein: 69g, Sugar: 9g, Potassium: 127mg, Sodium: 444mg

11.9 Lavender Buttermilk Bread

Preparation Time: 10 minutes
Cook Time: 3 hours
Servings: 1 loaf, 1.76 lb, 6 5/8 cups (and 2 tbsp), 800.84 g

Ingredients:

- water - ½ cup (125ml)
- buttermilk- 7/8 cup (207ml)
- olive oil - 1/4 cup (21ml)
- finely chopped fresh lavender leaves- 3 Tbsp (42g)
- Grated zest of 1 lemon
- finely chopped fresh lavender flowers - 1 ¼ tsp (8.4g)
- bread flour - 4 cups (544g)
- bread machine yeast - 2 3/4 tsp (9g)
- salt - 2 tsp (8.4g)

Preparation:

1. Add each ingredient to the bread machine in the order and at the temperature recommended by your bread machine manufacturer.
2. Close the lid, select the basic bread, medium crust setting on your bread machine and press start.
3. When the bread machine has finished baking, remove the bread and put it on a cooling rack.

Nutritional facts:

Calories: 170, Fat: 5g, Carbs: 27g, Protein: 2g, Sugar: 3g, Potassium: 99mg, Sodium: 245mg

11.10 Cajun and Tomato Bread

Preparation Time: 2 hours
Cook Time: 15 minutes
Servings: 1 loaf, 1.15 lb, 4 1/2 cups (and 1 tbsp), 522 g

Ingredients:

- water, ¾ cup (177ml) at 80°F to 90°F (26 degree C to 32 degree C)
- tomato paste- 1 tsp (5g)
- melted butter, cooled- 1 Tbsp (15g)
- salt- 1 tsp (5g)
- sugar- 1 Tbsp (15g)
- Cajun seasoning- ½ tbsp (7g)
- skim milk powder- 3 Tbsp (42g)
- white bread flour- 3 cups (360g)
- onion powder- ⅛ tsp (3g)
- bread machine or instant yeast- 1 tsp (5g)

Preparation:

1. As directed by the manufacturer, add the ingredients to your bread machine.
2. After setting the machine to make Basic/White bread, choose a light or medium crust and push Start.
3. After the loaf has finished baking, take the bucket out of the machine.
4. 5 minutes should pass as the loaf cools.
5. To release the loaf, gently shake the bucket. Then, turn the loaf over onto a cooling rack.

Nutritional facts:

Calories: 141, Fat: 2g, Carbs: 27g, Protein: 4g, Sugar: 4g, Potassium: 97mg, Sodium: 215mg

11.11 Rosemary Cranberry Pecan Bread

Preparation Time: 30 minutes
Cook Time: 3 hours
Servings: 1 loaf, 2.37 lb, 9 1/8 cups (and 1 tbsp), 1074.84 g

Ingredients:

- water, 1 1/3 cup (333ml) plus 2 Tbsp (30ml)
- butter- 2 Tbsp (30g)
- salt - 2 tsp (8.4g)
- bread flour - 4 cups (544g)
- dried sweetened cranberries - 3/4 cup (150g)
- non-fat powdered milk- 2 Tbsp (30g)
- toasted chopped pecans - 3/4 cup (150g)
- sugar - ¼ cups (59g)
- yeast - 2 tsp (8.4g)

Preparation:

1. Add each ingredient to the bread machine in the order and at the temperature recommended by your bread machine manufacturer.
2. Close the lid, select the basic bread, medium crust setting on your bread machine and press start.
3. When the bread machine has finished baking, remove the bread and put it on a cooling rack.

Nutritional facts:

Calories: 132, Fat: 5g, Carbs: 18g, Protein: 9g, Sugar: 3.89g, Potassium: 87mg, Sodium: 120mg

11.12 Chives Bread

Preparation Time: 3 hours 30 minutes
Cook Time: 15 minutes
Servings: 1 loaf, 1.17 lb, 4 1/2 cups (and 2 tbsp), 530.18 g

Ingredients:

- water, ¾ cup (177ml) at 80°F to 90°F (26 degree C to 32 degree C)
- sugar- 1 Tbsp (15g)
- melted butter, cooled- 1 Tbsp (15g)
- skim powder- 2 Tbsp (30g)
- salt- ¾ tsp (3.7g)
- garlic powder- 1/2 tsp (2.84g)
- minced chives- 1 Tbsp (15g)
- white bread flour- 3 cups (360g)
- cracked black pepper- 1/2 tsp (2.84g)
- bread machine or instant yeast- ¾ tsp (3.7g)

Preparation:

1. Follow the manufacturer's instructions when adding the ingredients to your bread machine.
2. Set the machine to produce basic/white bread. After choosing a light or medium crust, tap Start.
3. Take the bucket out of the machine once the loaf is finished baking.
4. Give the bread five minutes to cool.
5. Remove the loaf from the bucket with a gentle shake, then turn it out onto a cooling rack.

Nutritional facts:

Calories: 141, Fat: 2g, Carbs: 27g, Protein: 4g, Sugar: 1g, Potassium: 27mg, Sodium: 215mg

11.13 Saffron Tomato Bread

Preparation Time: 3 hours 30 minutes
Cook Time: 15 minutes | **Servings:** 1 loaf, 1.46 lb, 5 3/4 cups (and 1 tbsp), 663.84 g

Ingredients:

- bread machine yeast - 1 tsp (5g)
- panifarin - 1 Tbsp (15g)
- wheat bread machine flour - 2½ cup (313g)
- white sugar- 1½ Tbsp (23g)
- kosher salt – 1 1/2 tsp (6.84g)
- tomatoes, dried and chopped - 1 Tbsp (15g)
- extra-virgin olive oil - 2 Tbsp (30ml)
- firm cheese (cubes)- 1 Tbsp (15g)
- tomato paste - 1 Tbsp (15g)
- feta cheese - ½ cup (100g)
- serum- 1½ cup (188g)
- saffron - 1 pinch

Preparation:

1. Five minutes before cooking, pour in dried tomatoes and 1 Tbsp (15g) of olive oil. Add the tomato paste and mix.
2. Place all the dry and liquid ingredients, except additives, in the pan and follow the instructions for your bread machine.
3. Pay particular attention to measuring the ingredients. Use a measuring cup, measuring spoon, and kitchen scales to do so.
4. Set the baking program to BASIC and the crust type to MEDIUM.
5. Add the additives after the beep or place them in the dispenser of the bread machine.
6. Shake the loaf out of the pan. If necessary, use a spatula.
7. Wrap the bread with a kitchen towel and set it aside for an hour. Otherwise, you can cool it on a wire rack.

Nutritional facts:

Calories: 260, Fat: 9g, Carbs: 35g, Protein: 8g, Sugar: 5g, Potassium: 145mg, Sodium: 611mg

11.14 Potato Rosemary Loaf

Preparation Time: 5 minutes
Cook Time: 3 hours and 25 minutes
Servings: 1 loaf, 2.09 lb, 8 cups (and 1 tbsp), 949.4 g

Ingredients:

- wheat flour - 4 cups (544g)
- sunflower oil - 1 Tbsp (15ml)
- sugar - 1 Tbsp (15g)
- water - 1½ cup (375ml)
- salt – 1 1/2 tsp (8.4g)
- dry yeast - 1 tsp (5g)
- crushed rosemary to taste
- mashed potatoes, ground through a sieve - 1 cup (130g)

Preparation:

1. Add flour, salt, and sugar to the bread machine bucket and attach mixing paddle.
2. Add sunflower oil and water.
3. Put in yeast as directed.
4. Set the program of your bread machine to Bread with Filling mode and set crust type to Medium.
5. Once the bread machine beeps and signals to add more ingredients, open lid, add mashed potatoes, and chopped rosemary.
6. Wait until the cycle completes.
7. Once the loaf is ready, take the bucket out and allow loaf cool for 5 minutes.
8. Lightly shake the bucket to take out the loaf.

Nutritional facts:

Calories: 276, Fat: 3g, Carbs: 54g, Protein: 8g, Sugar: 1g, Potassium: 60mg, Sodium: 372mg

11.15 Cardamon Bread

Preparation Time: 2 hours
Cook Time: 15 minutes
Servings: 1 loaf, 1.08 lb, 4 1/8 cups (and 2 tbsp), 491.1 g

Ingredients:

- milk, ½ cup (125ml) at 80°F to 90°F (26 degree C to 32 degree C)
- egg, at room temperature- 1
- honey- 2 tsp (8.4ml)
- ground cardamom- 2/3 Tsp (3g)
- salt- 2/3 Tsp (3g)
- white bread flour- 3 cups (360g)
- melted butter, cooled- 1 tsp (5g)
- bread machine or instant yeast- ¾ tsp (3.7g)

Preparation:

1. According to the manufacturer's instructions, add the ingredients to your bread machine.
2. Set the breadmaker to make basic/white bread. Tap Start after selecting a light or medium crust.
3. Take the bucket out of the machine once the loaf is finished baking.
4. Give the bread five minutes to cool.
5. Remove the loaf from the bucket with a gentle shake, then turn it out onto a cooling rack.

Nutritional facts:

Calories: 149, Fat: 2g, Carbs: 29g, Protein: 5g, Sugar: 4g, Potassium: 76mg, Sodium: 211mg

11.16 Cumin Tossed Fancy Bread

Preparation Time: 5 minutes
Cook Time: 3 hours and 15 minutes
Servings: 1 loaf, 1.48 lb, 5 1/3 cups, 778 g

Ingredients:

- wheat flour - 5 1/3 cup (670g)
- sugar - 1½ tbsp (22g)
- salt – 1 1/2 tsp (8.4g)
- dry yeast - 1 Tbsp (15g)
- water - 1¾ cup (270ml)
- sunflower oil- 3 Tbsp (42g)
- cumin - 2 Tbsp (28.3g)

Preparation:

1. Add warm water to the bread machine bucket.
2. Add salt, sugar, and sunflower oil.
3. Sift in wheat flour and add yeast.
4. Set the program of your bread machine to French bread and set crust type to Medium.
5. Once the maker beeps, add cumin.
6. Wait until the cycle completes.
7. Once the loaf is ready, take the bucket out and let the loaf cool for 5 minutes.
8. Lightly shake the bucket to take out the loaf.

Nutritional facts: Calories: 368, Fat: 7g, Carbs: 67g, Protein: 9g, Sugar: 1g, Potassium: 89mg, Sodium: 192mg

12 HERB BREAD

12.1 Caramelized Onion Bread

Preparation Time: 15 minutes

Cook Time: 3 hours 35 minutes

Servings: 1 loaf, 0.86 lb, 3 1/20 cups and 1 tbsp, 391 g

Ingredients:

- butter - ½ tbsp (7g)
- water - 1 cup (130ml)
- onions, ½ cup (100g) sliced
- Gold Medal Better for Bread flour- 3 cups (360g)
- olive oil - 1 Tbsp (15ml)
- salt - 1 tsp (5g)
- Sugar- 2 Tbsp (30g)
- bread machine or quick active dry yeast - 1 ¼ tsp (8.4g)

Preparation:

1. Dissolve the butter over medium-low heat in a skillet.
2. Cook the onions in the butter for 10 to 15 minutes until they are brown and caramelized—then remove from the heat.
3. Add each ingredient except the onions to the bread machine in the order and at the temperature recommended by your bread machine manufacturer.
4. Close the lid, select the basic bread, medium crust setting on your bread machine, and press Start.
5. Add ½ cup (100g) of onions 5 to 10 minutes before the last kneading cycle ends.
6. When the bread machine has finished baking, remove the bread and put it on a cooling rack.

Nutritional facts: Calories: 160, Fat: 3g, Carbs: 30g, Protein: 4g, Sugar: 2g, Potassium: 27mg, Sodium: 192mg

12.2 Olive Bread

Preparation Time: 10 minutes

Cook Time: 3 hours

Servings: 1 loaf, 1.41 lb, 4 2/3 cups and 2 tbsp, 641 g

Ingredients:

- Brine from olive jar- ½ cup (100ml)
- Olive oil- 2 Tbsp (30ml)
- Warm water 43 degree C (110°F) to make 1 ½ cup (375ml) when combined with brine
- Bread flour- 3 cups (360g)
- Salt- 1 1/2 tsp (6.84g)
- Whole wheat flour- 1 2/3 cup (227g)
- Sugar- 2 Tbsp (30g) (28.3g)
- Dried leaf basil- 1 1/2 tsp (6.84g)
- Active dry yeast- 2 tsp (8.4g)
- Finely chopped kalamata olives- 2/3 cup (227g)

Preparation:

1. Add each ingredient except the olives to the bread machine in the order and at the temperature recommended by your bread machine manufacturer.
2. Close the lid, select the wheat, medium crust setting on your bread machine, and click Start.
3. Add the olives 10 minutes before the last kneading cycle ends.
4. When the bread machine has finished baking, remove the bread and put it on a cooling rack.

Nutritional facts: Calories: 141, Fat: 2g, Carbs: 29g, Protein: 5g, Sugar: 1g, Potassium: 89mg, Sodium: 245mg

12.3 Dilly Onion Bread

Preparation Time: 10 minutes

Cook Time: 3 hours and 5 minutes

Servings: 1 loaf, 0.59 lb, 2 1/3 cups and 1 tbsp, 270 g

Ingredients:

- Water- ¾ cup (150ml) 70°F (21 degrees C)
- Sugar- 2 Tbsp (30g)
- Butter, softened- 1 Tbsp (15g)
- Dried parsley flakes- 2 Tbsp (30g)
- Dried minced onion- 3 Tbsp (42g)
- Salt- 1 tsp (5g)
- Dill weed- 1 Tbsp (15g)
- Bread flour- 2 cups (240g)
- Garlic clove, minced- 1
- Nonfat dry milk powder- 1 Tbsp (15g)
- Whole wheat flour- 1/3 cup (113g)
- Active dry yeast serving- 2 tsp (8.4g)

Preparation:

1. Add each ingredient to the bread machine in the order and at the temperature recommended by your bread machine manufacturer.
2. Close the lid, select the basic bread, medium crust setting on your bread machine, and press Start.
3. When the bread machine has finished baking, remove the bread and put it on a cooling rack.

Nutritional facts: Calories: 78, Fat: 1g, Carbs: 17g, Protein: 3g, Sugar: 1g, Potassium: 27mg, Sodium: 192mg

12.4 Cardamom Cranberry Bread

Preparation Time: 5 minutes

Cook Time: 3 hours

Servings: 1 loaf, 1.65 lb, 5 1/4 cups, 748 g

Ingredients:

- Water- 1¾ cup (270ml)
- Salt- 1 1/2 tsp (6.84g)
- Brown sugar- 2 Tbsp (30g)
- Flour- 4 cups (544g)
- Coconut oil- 2 Tbsp (30g)
- Cardamom- 2 tsp (8.4g)
- Cinnamon- 2 tsp (8.4g)
- Yeast- 2 tsp (8.4g)
- Dried cranberries- 1 cup (130g)

Preparation:

1. Add each ingredient except the dried cranberries to the bread machine in the order and at the temperature recommended by your bread machine manufacturer.
2. Close the lid, select the basic bread, medium crust setting on your bread machine, and press Start.
3. Add the dried cranberries 5 to 10 minutes before the last kneading cycle ends.
4. When the bread machine has finished baking, remove the bread and put it on a cooling rack.

Nutritional facts:

Calories: 157, Fat: 3g, Carbs: 4g, Protein: 3g, Sugar: 2g, Potassium: 27mg, Sodium: 272mg

12.5 Original Italian Herb Bread

Preparation Time: 2 hours 40 minutes
Cook Time: 50 minutes
Servings: 2 loaves, 2.98 lb each, 5 1/3 cups each, 1350 g total (675 g each)

Ingredients:

- Water at 80 degrees F (26 degrees C)- 1 cup (237ml)
- Butter- 1½ tbsp (22g)
- Olive brine- ½ cup (100ml)
- Salt- 1 tsp (5g)
- Sugar- 3 Tbsp (42g)
- Flour- 5 1/3 cup (675g)
- Bread machine yeast- 1 tsp (5g)
- Olives, black/green- 20
- Italian herbs- 1 1/2 tsp (8.4g)

Preparation:

1. Cut olives into slices.
2. Put the ingredients in your bread machine (except olives), carefully following the instructions of the manufacturer.
3. Set the program of your bread machine to French bread and set crust type to Medium.
4. Press START.
5. Once the maker beeps, add olives.
6. Wait until the cycle completes.
7. Once the loaf is ready, take the bucket out and allow loaf cool for 5 minutes.
8. Lightly shake the bucket to take out the loaf.
9. Transfer to a cooling rack, slice, and serve.

Nutritional facts:

Calories: 386, Fat: 7g, Carbs: 71g, Protein: 10g, Sugar: 1g, Potassium: 156mg, Sodium: 592mg

12.6 Herbed Pesto Bread

Preparation Time: 5 minutes
Cook Time: 50 minutes
Servings: 1 loaf, 0.67 lb, 2 1/4 cups and 1/2 tbsp, 304 g

Ingredients:

- water, 2/3 cup (158ml) at 80°F to 90°F (26 degree C to 32 degree C)
- minced garlic- 1 tsp (5g)
- melted butter, cooled- 1½ tbsp (22g)
- salt- ¾ tsp (3.7g)
- sugar- ½ tbsp (7g)
- chopped fresh basil- ¾ tsp (3.7g)
- chopped fresh parsley- 2 Tbsp (30g)
- white bread flour- 2 cups (240g)
- grated Parmesan cheese- ¼ cups (59g)
- bread machine or active dry yeast- ¾ tsp (3.7g)

Preparation:

1. As directed by the manufacturer, add the ingredients to your breadmaker.
2. Select a light or medium crust, program the machine for Basic/White bread, and then click Start.
3. After the loaf has finished baking, take the bucket out of the machine.
4. Give the bread five minutes to cool.
5. Remove the loaf from the bucket with a gentle shake, then turn it out onto a cooling rack.

Nutritional facts:

Calories: 149, Fat: 3g, Carbs: 25g, Protein: 5g, Sugar: 0.23g, Potassium: 56mg, Sodium: 243mg

12.7 Chive Bread

Preparation Time: 10 minutes
Cook Time: 3 hours
Servings: 1 loaf, 0.97 lb, 3 1/4 cups and 1/2 tbsp, 440 g

Ingredients:

- milk (70°F) 21 degrees C- ¾ tsp (3.7ml)
- sour cream- ¼ cups (59g)
- water (70°F) 21 degrees C- ¼ cups (59ml)
- sugar -1 1/2 tsp (2.84g)
- butter - 2 Tbsp (30g)
- bread flour- 3 cups (360g)
- salt - 1 1/2 tsp (2.84g)
- minced chives- ¼ cups (59g)
- baking soda - ⅛ tsp (1.2g)
- active dry yeast leaves - 2 ¼ tsp (8.4g)

Preparation:

1. Add each ingredient to the bread machine in the order and at the temperature recommended by your bread machine manufacturer.
2. Close the lid, select the basic bread, medium crust setting on your bread machine, and press Start.
3. When the bread machine has finished baking, remove the bread and put it on a cooling rack.

Nutritional facts:

Calories: 105, Fat: 18g, Carbs: 18g, Protein: 4g, Sugar: 2g, Potassium: 87mg, Sodium: 282mg

12.8 Pumpkin Cinnamon Bread

Preparation Time: 10 minutes
Cook Time: 3 hours
Servings: 1 loaf, 0.98 lb, 2 1/3 cups and 1 tbsp, 445 g

Ingredients:

- canned pumpkin- 1 cup (130g)
- eggs- 2
- vanilla- 1 tsp (5g)
- baking powder- 2 tsp (8.4g)
- all-purpose bread flour- 1 ½ cup (188g)
- vegetable oil - 1/3 cup (113ml)
- salt - ¼ tsp (8.4g)
- ground nutmeg- ¼ tsp (8.4g)
- ground cloves- ⅛ tsp (2.84g)
- sugar - 1 cup (130g)
- ground cinnamon - ¼ tsp (8.4g)

Preparation:

1. Add each ingredient to the bread machine in the order and at the temperature recommended by your bread machine manufacturer.
2. Close the lid, select the quick, medium crust setting on your bread machine, and click Start.
3. When the bread machine has finished baking, remove the bread and put it on a cooling rack.

Nutritional facts:

Calories: 140, Fat: 5g, Carbs: 39g, Protein: 3g, Sugar: 5g, Potassium: 46mg, Sodium: 282mg

12.9 Garlic Bread

Preparation Time: 2 hours 10 minutes
Cook Time: 30 minutes
Servings: 1 loaf, approx. 1.6 lb, approx. 3 1/4 cups (plus 2 tbsp), approx. 725g

Ingredients:

- Water- 1 1/4 cups (295 ml)
- Olive oil- 2 Tbsp (30 ml)
- White sugar- 1 tsp (4g)
- Bread flour- 3 1/4 cups (390g)
- Salt- 1 tsp (6g)
- Dried basil- 1 tsp (1g)
- Minced garlic- 1 Tbsp (9g)
- Grated Parmesan cheese- 1/4 cup (25g)
- Fresh chives, finely chopped- 2 Tbsp (6g)
- Garlic powder- 1/2 tsp (1.5g)
- Coarsely ground black pepper- 1/2 tsp (1g)
- Active dry yeast or bread machine yeast- 2 1/4 tsp (7g)

Preparation:

1. Follow the manufacturer's instructions for the order in which ingredients should be added to the bread machine pan. Usually, it's recommended to add liquids first, followed by dry ingredients, with yeast added last.
2. Choose the Basic or White Bread cycle on your bread machine and press the Start button. This cycle usually includes time for kneading, rising, and baking the bread.
3. Once the bread is done, carefully remove it from the bread machine and allow it to cool on a wire rack for at least 10-15 minutes before slicing. This helps the bread maintain its structure.
4. Optional: For an extra garlic flavor, you can mix 2 Tbsp of melted butter with 1 tsp of garlic powder and brush it over the top of the bread once it's out of the machine.

Nutritional facts:

Calories: 189, Fat: 4g, Carbs: 31g, Protein: 6g, Sugar: 1g, Potassium: 55mg, Sodium: 235mg

12.10 Inspiring Cinnamon Bread

Preparation Time: 15 minutes
Cook Time: 2 hours and 15 minutes
Servings: 1 loaf, approx. 0.58 lb, 2 3/4 cups, 263g

Ingredients:

- Milk, 2/3 cup (158ml) at 80 degrees F (26 degrees C)
- melted butter, cooled - 3 Tbsp (42g)
- whole egg, beaten- 1
- salt - 1/3 tsp (15g)
- sugar- 1/3 cup (113g)
- white bread flour - 2 cups (240g)
- ground cinnamon - 1 tsp (5g)
- active dry yeast - 1 1/3 tsp (15g)

Preparation:

1. Put the ingredients to your bread machine, carefully following the instructions of the manufacturer.
2. Set the program of your bread machine to Basic/White Bread and set crust type to Medium.
3. Wait until the cycle completes.
4. Once the loaf is ready, take the bucket out and allow the loaf to cool for 5 minutes.
5. Remove the loaf.

Nutritional facts: Calories: 198, Fat: 5g, Carbs: 34g, Protein: 5g, Sugar: 5g, Potassium: 84mg, Sodium: 321mg

12.11 Herbal Garlic Cream Cheese Delight

Preparation Time: 5 minutes
Cook Time: 2 hours and 45 minutes
Servings: 1 loaf, approx. 0.55 lb, 2 2/3 cups, 250g

Ingredients:

- Water, 1/3 cup (113ml) at 80 degrees F (26 degrees C)
- whole egg, beaten, at room temp- 1
- herb and garlic cream cheese mix, at room temp- 1/3 cup (113g)
- sugar- 1 Tbsp (15g)
- melted butter, cooled - 4 tsp (24ml)
- white bread flour - 2 cups (240g)
- salt - 2/3 tsp (15g)
- instant yeast - 1 tsp (5g)

Preparation:

1. Put the ingredients in your bread machine, carefully following the instructions of the manufacturer.
2. Set the program of your bread machine to Basic/White Bread and set crust type to Medium.
3. Wait until the cycle completes.
4. Once the loaf is ready, take the bucket out and allow loaf to cool for 5 minutes.
5. Lightly shake the bucket to take out the loaf.

Nutritional facts:

Calories: 182, Fat: 6g, Carbs: 27g, Protein: 5g, Sugar: 1g, Potassium: 27mg, Sodium: 242mg

12.12 Dill And Rosemary Herb Bread

Preparation Time: 1 hour 20 minutes
Cook Time: 50 minutes
Servings: 1 loaf, approx. 0.87 lb, 3 1/4 cups (plus 1 tbsp), 395g

Ingredients:

- Milk- 3/4 cup (177ml)
- Salt- 1 tsp (5g)
- Sugar- 1 Tbsp (15g)
- chopped onion- 1/3 cup (113g)
- butter or margarine- 1 Tbsp (15g)
- Dried dill- 1/2 tsp (2.84g)
- bread flour- 3 cups (360g)
- Dried rosemary- 1/2 tsp (8.4g)
- Dried basil- 1/2 tsp (8.4g)
- Active dry yeast - 1 1/2 tsp (8g)

Preparation:

1. Place the ingredients in the bread pan. Select medium crus then the rapid bake cycle. Press starts.
2. After 5-10 minutes, observe the dough as it kneads, if you hear straining sounds in your machine or if the dough appears stiff and dry, add 1 Tbsp (15g) Liquid at a time until the dough becomes smooth, pliable, soft, and slightly tacky to the touch.
3. Take out the bread from the pan after baking. Place on rack and allow to cool for 1 hour before slicing.

Nutritional facts:

Calories: 66, Fat: 0g, Carbs: 15g, Protein: 2g, Sugar: 1g, Potassium: 27mg, Sodium: 192mg

12.13 Sesame French Bread

Preparation Time: 20 minutes
Cook Time: 3 hours 15 minutes
Servings: 1 loaf, approx. 0.87 lb, 3 1/4 cups (plus 2 tbsp), 395g

Ingredients:

- water - 7/8 cup (207ml)
- bread flour - 3 cups (360g)
- butter, softened- 1 Tbsp (15g)
- salt - 1 tsp (5g)
- sugar - 2 tsp (8.4g)
- sesame seeds toasted - 2 Tbsp (30g)
- yeast - 2 tsp (8.4g)

Preparation:

1. Add each ingredient to the bread machine in the order and at the temperature recommended by your bread machine manufacturer.
2. Close the lid, select the French bread, medium crust setting on your bread machine and press start.
3. When the bread machine has finished baking, remove the bread and put it on a cooling rack.

Nutritional facts:

Calories: 180, Fat: 3g, Carbs: 28g, Protein: 6g, Sugar: 3g, Potassium: 68mg, Sodium: 290mg

12.14 Cinnamon & Dried Fruits Bread

PrepTime: 5 min | **Cook Time:** 3 hours
Servings: 1 loaf, approx. 1.07 lb, 4 cups (plus 3 tbsp), 485g

Ingredients:

- flour - 2¾ cup (344g)
- sugar - 4 tbsp (56g)
- dried fruits - 1½ cup (188g)
- milk powder - 1 Tbsp (15g)
- butter - 2½ tbsp (45g)
- ground nutmeg- 1/2 tsp (2.84g)
- cinnamon- 1 tsp (5g)
- peanuts - ½ cup (100g)
- vanillin - ¼ tsp (8.4g)
- salt - 1 tsp (5g)
- powdered sugar, for sprinkling
- bread machine yeast – 1 1/2 tsp (8g)

Preparation:

1. Put the ingredients in your bread machine (except peanuts and powdered sugar), carefully following the instructions of the manufacturer.
2. Set the program of your bread machine to Basic/White Bread and set crust type to Medium.
3. Once the bread machine beeps, moisten dough with a bit of water and add peanuts.
4. Wait until the cycle completes.
5. Once the loaf is ready, take the bucket out and allow bread cool for 5 minutes.
6. Lightly shake the bucket to take out the bread.
7. Sprinkle with powdered sugar.

Nutritional facts: Calories: 315, Fat: 4g, Carbs: 65g, Protein: 5g, Sugar: 1g, Potassium: 124mg, Sodium: 492mg

12.15 Italian Ciabatta Bread

Preparation Time: 5 minutes

Cook Time: 3 hours 5 minutes

Servings: 1 loaf, approx. 1.31 lb, 4 3/4 cups (plus 3 tbsp), 595g

Ingredients:

- margarine - 2 Tbsp (30g)
- water - 1 ½ cup (188ml)
- sugar - 2 Tbsp (30g)
- dried marjoram - 1 1/2 tsp (6.84g)
- powdered milk - 3 Tbsp (42g)
- salt - 1 1/2 tsp (6.84g)
- dried basil - 1 1/2 tsp (6.84g)
- yeast - 1 ¼ tsp (8.4g)
- bread flour- 4 cups (544g)
- dried thyme - 1 1/2 tsp (6.84g)

Preparation:

1. Add each ingredient to the bread machine in the order and at the temperature recommended by your bread machine manufacturer.
2. Close the lid, select the basic bread, medium crust setting on your bread machine, and press Start.
3. When the bread machine has finished baking, remove the bread and put it on a cooling rack.

Nutritional facts:

Calories: 120, Fat: 3g, Carbs: 4g, Protein: 4g, Sugar: 2g, Potassium: 65mg, Sodium: 292mg

12.16 Onion and Garlic Bread

Preparation Time: 10 minutes

Cook Time: 2 hours 10 minutes

Servings: 1 loaf, approx. 0.67 lb, 3 cups, 304g

Ingredients:

- water - ½ cup (100ml)
- chopped green bell pepper - ¼ cups (59g)
- chopped onion - ¼ cups (59g)
- soft butter - 2 tsp (8.4g)
- finely chopped garlic- 2 tsp (8.4g)
- sugar - 1 Tbsp (15g)
- bread flour - 2 cups (240g)
- salt- 1/2 tsp (2.84g)
- Cajun - 1 tsp (5g)
- active dry yeast- 1 tsp (5g)

Preparation:

1. Add each ingredient to the bread machine in the order and at the temperature recommended by your bread machine manufacturer.
2. Close the lid, select the basic bread, medium crust setting on your bread machine, and press Start.
3. When the bread machine has finished baking, remove the bread and put it on a cooling rack.

Nutritional facts: Calories: 151, Fat: 4g, Carbs: 24g, Protein: 5g, Sugar: 1g, Potassium: 66mg, Sodium: 234mg

13 VEGETABLE BREAD

13.1 Cauliflower and Garlic Bread

Preparation Time: 10 minutes
Cook Time: 4 hours | **Servings:** 1 loaf, 0.95 lb, 3 7/8 cups (3 cups and 14 tbsp), 750g

Ingredients:

- eggs, 5 separated
- rice cauliflower - 1 1/2 cup (360g)
- coconut flour- 2/3 cup (227g)
- sea salt - 1/2 tsp (2.84g)
- garlic, minced- 1 tsp (5g)
- parsley, chopped - 1/2 Tbsp (30g)
- rosemary, chopped- 1/2 Tbsp (30g)
- unsalted butter- 3 Tbsp (42g)
- baking powder- 3/4 tbsp (56g)

Preparation:

1. Place the cauliflower rice in a bowl and cover it. Microwave for 3–4 minutes or until steaming. Then drain. Wrap in cheesecloth and remove as much moisture as possible. Set aside.
2. Place egg whites in a mixing container and whisk until stiff peaks form.
3. Then transfer 1/4 of the whipped egg whites into a food processor. Add remaining ingredients except for cauliflower and pulse for 2 minutes until blended.
4. Add cauliflower rice, and pulse for 2 minutes until combined. Then pulse in the remaining egg whites until just mixed.
5. Add batter into the bread bucket and cover. Select the BASIC/WHITE cycle. Press START.
6. Remove the bread when done. Cool, slice, and serve.

Nutritional facts: Calories: 105, Fat: 6g, Carbs: 2g, Protein: 9g, Sugar: 1g, Potassium: 86mg, Sodium: 211mg

13.2 Vegetable Loaf

Preparation Time: 10 minutes
Cook Time: 4 hours
Servings: 1 loaf, 1.36 lb, 5 1/8 cups (5 cups and 2 tbsp), 618g

Ingredients:

- Eggs- 4
- medium zucchini, grated- 1
- coconut oil- 1/4 cup (21ml)
- small carrot, grated- 1
- pumpkin, grated - 1 cup (130g)
- almond flour- 1 cup (130g)
- coconut flour- 1/3 cup (113g)
- flaxseeds - 2 Tbsp (30g)
- sesame seeds- 2 Tbsp (30g)
- sunflower seeds- 2 Tbsp (30g)
- salt- 2 tsp (8.4g)
- psyllium husks- 2 Tbsp (30g)
- pumpkin seeds- 2 Tbsp (30g)
- cumin, ground- 2 tsp (8.4g)
- smoked paprika - 1 Tbsp (14g)
- baking powder - 2 tsp (8.4g)

Preparation:

1. Beat the eggs till frothy, beat in the oil, and then stir in zucchini, pumpkin, and carrot until just mixed. Place flour in another bowl. Then stir in the remaining ingredients until mixed.
2. Add egg mixture into the bread bucket, top with flour mixture, and cover.
3. Select the BASIC/WHITE cycle. Press START. Remove the bread when done. Cool, slice, and serve.

Nutritional facts:

Calories: 178, Fat: 12g, Carbs: 5g, Protein: 8g, Sugar: 1g, Potassium: 69mg, Sodium: 289mg

13.3 Almond Pumpkin Bread

Preparation Time: 10 minutes
Cook Time: 60 minutes
Servings: 1 loaf, 1.77 lb, 6 7/8 cups (6 cups and 14 tbsp), 804g

Ingredients:

- oil - 1/3 cup (113ml)
- pumpkin puree, canned - 1 1/2 cup (360g)
- large eggs- 3
- baking powder - 1 1/2 tsp (8.4g)
- granulated sugar - 1 cup (130g)
- salt - 1/4 tsp (1.42g)
- baking soda- 1/2 tsp (2.84g)
- nutmeg, ground- 1/4 tsp (1.42g)
- cinnamon, ground- 3/4 tsp(3.42g)
- almond flour- 3 cups (360g)
- ginger, ground- 1/4 tsp (1.42g)
- pecans, chopped- 1/2 cup (100g)

Preparation:

1. Grease the bread machine pan with cooking spray. Stir all the wet ingredients in a bowl. Add all the dry ingredients except pecans until mixed.
2. Pour the batter onto the bread machine pan and place it back inside the bread machine. Close and select QUICK BREAD. Add the pecans after the beep. Remove the bread when done. Cool, slice, and serve.

Nutritional facts:

Calories: 52, Fat: 12g, Carbs: 5g, Protein: 11g, Sugar: 1g, Potassium: 57mg, Sodium: 126mg

13.4 Celery Bread

Preparation Time: 10 minutes
Cook Time: 3 hours
Servings: 1 loaf, 1.20 lb, 4 5/8 cups (4 cups and 10 tbsp), 545g

Ingredients:

- cream of celery soup- 1 can 10 oz (283g)
- vegetable oil- 1 Tbsp (14ml)
- low-fat milk, heated- 3 Tbsp (42ml)
- celery, fresh, sliced thin- 3/4 cup (150g)
- celery, garlic, or onion salt- 1 1/4 tsp (1.42g)
- egg- 1
- celery leaves, fresh and chopped - 1 Tbsp (14g)
- sugar- 1/4 tsp (1.42g)
- bread flour- 3 cups (360g)
- ginger- 1/4 tsp (1.42g)
- quick-cooking oats- 1/2 cup (100g)
- gluten- 2 Tbsp (30g)
- celery seeds- 2 tsp (8.4g)
- active dry yeast- 1 package

Preparation:

1. Add all ingredients to the bread machine. Select the basic bread setting.
2. Remove the bread when done. Cool, slice, and serve.

Nutritional facts:

Calories: 70, Fat: 2g, Carbs: 7g, Protein: 4g, Sugar: 1g, Potassium: 27mg, Sodium: 125mg

13.5 Keto Almond Bread

Preparation Time: 25 minutes
Cook Time: 2 hours |
Servings: 1 loaf, 1.45 lb, 5 5/8 cups (5 cups and 10 tbsp), 659g

Ingredients:

- water - 1 1/2 cup (320ml)
- unsalted butter- 2 Tbsp (30g)+2 tsp (8.4g)
- salt- 1 1/2 tsp (8.4g)
- sugar- 1 Tbsp (14g)+1 tsp (5g)
- non-fat dry milk- 2 Tbsp (30ml)+2 tsp (8.4ml)
- almond flour- 4 cups (544g)
- active dry yeast - 2 tsp (8.4g)
- dry onion soup mix - 4 tbsp (56g)

Preparation:

1. Add all ingredients except dry onion soup mix in the bread machine pan.
2. Close the lid. Select BASIC cycle on the bread machine and then press START.
3. The machine will ping after around 30–40 minutes.
4. Pause the bread machine and add the dry onion soup mix.
5. Press START again and allow the cycle to continue. Once the loaf is finished, transfer it to a cooling rack.
6. Slice and serve with cream cheese or butter or as a soup side dish.

Nutritional facts:

Calories: 326, Fat: 14g, Carbs: 38g, Protein: 7g, Sugar: 1g, Potassium: 54mg, Sodium: 492mg

13.6 Sundried Tomato Bread

Preparation Time: 10 minutes
Cook Time: 2 hours |
Servings: 1 loaf, 0.71 lb, 2 7/8 cups (2 cups and 14 tbsp), 324g

Ingredients:

- flour - 2 1/4 cup (21g)
- kosher salt - 1 tsp (5g)
- baking powder - 1 Tbsp (14g)
- buttermilk- 1 1/2 cup (320ml)
- large eggs- 3
- basil, dried- 1 Tbsp (14g)
- canola oil - 6 tbsp (85ml)
- Sundried Tomato Roughly, Chopped- 1 cup (130g)

Preparation:

1. Place all the fixings in the bread machine bucket except for basil and sundried tomato.
2. Secure the lid cover. Select the QUICK BREAD setting on the bread machine, then press START.
3. Wait for the ping, fruit, and nut signal to open the lid, and add the basil and sundried tomato. Place a cover and press START to continue. When the cycle finishes, transfer the loaf to a wire rack and let it cool.
4. Slice and serve.

Nutritional facts:

Calories: 180, Fat: 4g, Carbs: 30g, Protein: 3g, Sugar: 1g, Potassium: 97mg, Sodium: 234mg

13.7 Onion Bread

Preparation Time: 20 minutes
Cook Time: 5 minutes | **Servings:** 1 loaf, 0.73 lb, 2 5/8 cups (2 cups and 10 tbsp), 330g

Ingredients:

- Red onion, 1 diced and sautéed with 1/2 tsp (2.84g) butter until golden brown
- salt - 1/4 tsp (1.42g)
- unsalted butter, melted- 3 tsp (15g)
- psyllium husk flour - 3 tsp (15g)
- garlic, ground - 1/4 tsp (1.42g)
- baking powder- 1/2 tsp (2.84g)
- eggs - 5
- onion powder- 1/2 tsp (2.84g)
- active dry yeast - 3/4 tsp (3.84g)
- flour - 1 cup (130g)

Preparation:

1. Get a mixing container and combine the flour, salt, psyllium husk flour, ground onion, baking powder, and ground garlic.
2. Get another mixing container and mix the melted unsalted butter, eggs, and sautéed onions.
3. As per the instructions in the machine manual, pour the ingredients into the bread pan and follow the yeast instructions.
4. Put bread pan in the machine, and select the basic bread setting - together with the bread size and crust type if available - then press start once you have closed the lid of the machine.
5. When the bread is ready, extract it, and place it on a metallic mesh surface to cool completely before cutting and eating it.

Nutritional facts:

Calories: 124, Fat: 9g, Carbs: 1g, Protein: 9g, Sugar: 1g, Potassium: 78mg, Sodium: 211mg

13.8 Tomato Bread

Preparation Time: 15 minutes
Cook Time: 45 minutes | **Servings:** 1 loaf, 0.61 lb, 2 1/8 cups (2 cups and 2 tbsp), 278g

Ingredients:

- whole eggs- 4
- flaxseed meal - 1 cup (130g)
- salted butter, melted- 2 Tbsp (30g)
- baking powder - 2 tsp (8.4g)
- oat fiber - 4 tsp (16g)
- sea salt - 1/4 tsp (1.42g)
- xanthan gum- 1 1/2 tsp (6.84g)
- garlic powder- 1/4 tsp (1.42g)
- basil, dried- 1/2 tsp (2.84g)
- parmesan, grated- 1/4 cup (21g)
- sun-dried tomatoes, diced- 2 Tbsp (30g)

Preparation:

1. Carefully whisk eggs and butter together. Pour all the ingredients into the bread machine pan.
2. Close the lid. Set the bread machine program to CAKE for 30–45 minutes (depending on the bread machine model) and choose the crust color LIGHT. Press START. Help the bread machine knead the dough with a spatula, if necessary. Before the baking cycle begins, sprinkle the top with grated parmesan.
3. After baking for 20 minutes, check for doneness with a toothpick. Wait until the program is complete, then take the bucket out and let it cool for 5–10 minutes.
4. Shake the loaf from the pan and let it cool for 30 minutes on a cooling rack.
5. Slice and serve.

Nutritional facts:

Calories: 87, Fat: 5.1g, Carbs: 2.2g, Protein: 3g, Sugar: 1g, Potassium: 27mg, Sodium: 112mg

13.9 Beetroot Bread

Preparation Time: 30 minutes
Cook Time: 45 minutes | **Servings:** 2 loaves, 1.28 lb, 6 and 1/3 cups, 582.08 g

Ingredients:

- fresh beetroot, grated- 1 cup (130g)
- coconut flour- 1/2 cup (100g)
- almond flour - 1 cup (130g)
- cinnamon, ground- 1/4 tsp (1.42g)
- nutmeg, ground- 1/2 tsp (2.84g)
- Swerve sweetener- 1/3 cup (113g)
- active dry yeast- 2 tsp (8.4g)
- unsalted butter, melted- 4 tsp
- warm water - 1/2 cup (125ml)
- baking powder - 1 tsp (5g)
- walnuts, roasted and sliced- 1/3 cup (113g)
- salt - 1/4 tsp (1.42g)

Preparation:

1. Get a mixing container and combine the almond flour, coconut flour, roasted walnuts, Swerve sweetener, cinnamon ground, nutmeg powder, and baking powder.
2. Get another container and combine the warm water, shredded beetroot, and melted unsalted butter.
3. As per the instructions in the machine manual, pour the ingredients in the bread pan, taking care to follow how to mix in the yeast.
4. In the machine, place the bread pan, select the sweet bread setting - together with the crust type if available - then press start once you have closed the lid of the machine.
5. When the bread is ready, remove the bread pan from the machine using oven mitts. Use a stainless spatula to extract the bread from the pan and place the bread on a metallic rack to cool before slicing it.

Nutritional facts: Calories: 852, Fat: 41g, Carbs: 43g, Protein: 23g, Sugar: 11g, Potassium: 227mg, Sodium: 1192mg

13.10 Carrot Bread

PrepTime: 20 Mins | Cook Time: 1 h 15 min
Servings: 1 loaf, 0.76 lb, 4 cups, 344.4 g

Ingredients:

- all-purpose flour - 2 cups (240g)
- baking powder - 1 1/2 tsp (8.4g)
- baking soda - 1/2 tsp (2.84g)
- salt - 1/2 tsp (2.84g)
- ground cinnamon - 1 tsp (2.8g)
- ground nutmeg - 1/2 tsp (2.84g)
- granulated sugar - 1/2 cup (100g)
- brown sugar - 1/2 cup (100g)
- vegetable oil - 1/2 cup (120ml)
- eggs - 3 large
- vanilla sugar - 1 Tbsp (15g)
- grated carrots - 2 cups (200g)
- chopped walnuts or pecans (optional) - 1/2 cup (60g)

Preparation:

1. Preheat the oven to 350°F (175°C). Grease and flour a 9x5-inch loaf pan.
2. In a large mixing bowl, whisk together the flour, baking powder, baking soda, salt, cinnamon, and nutmeg.
3. In a separate bowl, whisk together the granulated sugar, brown sugar, vegetable oil, eggs, and vanilla extract until well combined.
4. Pour the wet ingredients into the dry ingredients and stir until just combined. Fold in the grated carrots and chopped nuts, if using.
5. Pour the batter into the prepared loaf pan and smooth the top.
6. Bake for 1 hour to 1 hour 15 minutes, or until a toothpick inserted into the center comes out clean.
7. Remove from the oven and let the bread cool in the pan for 10 minutes. Then

transfer to a wire rack to cool completely.

Nutritional facts: Calories: 235, Fat: 11g, Carbs: 31g, Protein: 4g, Sugar: 16g, Sodium: 260mg, Fiber: 2g

13.11 Zucchini Bread

Preparation Time: 2h 10 Mins
Servings: 1 loaf, 0.80 lb, 4 and 1/4 cups, 362.54g

Ingredients:

- Eggs- 2
- oil - 1 cup (130ml)
- salt - ¼ tsp (8.4g)
- vanilla sugar - 1 Tbsp (15g)
- white sugar- 1 cup (130g)
- nuts, ground - ½ cup (100g)
- cinnamon - 2 tsp (8.4g)
- baking powder- 1 Tbsp (15g)
- all-purpose flour, well sifted- 3 cups (360g)
- Zucchini, Grated- 1¼ cups (59g)

Preparation:

1. Follow the manufacturer's instructions and put the ingredients in the bread machine (except the zucchini).
2. Set the program of the bread machine to CAKE/SWEET and set the crust type to LIGHT.
3. Press START. Once the machine beeps, add zucchini. When the cycle is completed, take the bucket out and allow bread cool for 5 minutes.
4. Shake the bucket gently to take out the loaf, then transfer to a cooling rack, slice, and serve.

Nutritional facts:

Calories: 555, Fat: 30g, Carbs: 62g, Protein: 9g, Sugar: 1g, Potassium: 127mg, Sodium: 322mg

13.12 Pumpkin Bread

Preparation Time: 10 minutes
Cook Time: 4 hours
Servings: 1 loaf (12 slices), 0.86 lb, 2 and 2/3 cups, 389.6 g

Ingredients:

- eggs, pasteurized- 2
- sugar - 2/3 cup (227g)
- butter- 1 cup (130g)
- cloves, ground- 1/8 tsp (0.61g)
- pumpkin puree- 2/3 cup (227g)
- ginger, ground- 1/8 tsp (0.61g)
- cinnamon, ground- 1/2 tsp (2.84g)
- nutmeg, ground- 1/2 tsp (2.84g)
- baking powder - 1 tsp (5g)

Preparation:

1. Take a large bowl, crack eggs, and then beat the remaining ingredients in the order described in the ingredients until incorporated.
2. Add batter into the bread bucket, shut the lid, select the basic/white cycle setting and then press the UP/DOWN arrow button to adjust baking time according to the bread machine; it will take 3–4 hours.
3. Then press the crust button to select light crust if available, and press the START/STOP button to switch on the bread machine.
4. When the bread machine beeps, open the lid, take out the bread basket, and lift the bread.
5. Let bread cool on for one hour, then cut it into 12 slices and serve.

Nutritional facts: Calories: 148, Fat: 12g, Carbs: 7g, Protein: 6g, Sugar: 1g, Potassium: 89mg, Sodium: 321mg

14 MEAT BREAD

14.1 Ham Bread

Preparation Time: 30-45 minutes

Cook Time: 2 hours

Servings: 1 loaf (8 servings), 2.14 lb, 6 and 2/3 cups, 973 g

Ingredients:

- wheat flour - 3 1/3 cup (400g)
- milk powder- ½ cup (100g)
- ham- 1 cup (130g)
- fresh yeast- 1 tsp (5g)
- sugar - 1 ½ tbsp
- dried basil- 1 tsp (5g)
- salt - 1 tsp (5g)
- olive oil- 2 Tbsp (30g)
- water - 1 1/3 cup (333g)

Preparation:

1. Cut ham into cubes of 0.5-1 cm (approximately ¼ inch).
2. Put all ingredients in the bread machine from the following order: water, olive oil, salt, sugar, flour, milk powder, ham, and yeast.
3. Put all the ingredients according to the instructions in your bread machine.
4. Basil put in a dispenser or fill it later, at the signal in the container.
5. Turn on the bread machine.
6. After the end of the baking cycle, leave the bread container In the bread machine to keep warm for 1 hour.
7. Then your delicious bread is ready!

Nutritional facts:

Calories: 287, Fat: 5g, Carbs: 47g, Protein: 11g, Sugar: 6g, Potassium: 167mg, Sodium: 557mg

14.2 Meat Bread

Preparation Time: 1 hour 30 minutes

Cook Time: 1 hour 30 minutes

Servings: 1 loaf (8 servings), 1.65 lb, 5 cups, 750g

Ingredients:

- boiled chicken- 2 cups (240g)
- milk- 1 cup (250ml)
- dry yeast- 1 Tbsp (15g)
- flour- 3 cups (360g)
- sugar - 1 tsp (5g)
- egg - 1
- oil - 2 Tbsp (30ml)
- salt- ½ tbsp

Preparation:

1. Pre-cook the meat. You can use a leg or fillet.
2. Separate meat from the bone and cut it into small pieces.
3. Pour all ingredients into the bread machine according to the instructions.
4. Add chicken pieces now.
5. The program is Basic.
6. This bread is perfectly served with dill and butter.

Nutritional facts:

Calories: 283, Fat: 6g, Carbs: 38g, Protein: 17g, Sugar: 2g, Potassium: 127mg, Sodium: 484mg

14.3 Onion Bacon Bread

Preparation Time: 1 hour 30 minutes
Cook Time: 1 hour 30 minutes
Servings: 1 loaf (8 servings), 2.15 lb, 8 and 1/3 cups, 974.4 g

Ingredients:

- water - 1 ½ cup (375ml)
- dry yeast - 3 tsp (15g)
- sugar - 2 Tbsp (30g)
- flour- 4 ½ cup (640g)
- salt - 2 tsp (8.4g)
- egg - 1
- small onions, chopped- 3
- oil - 1 Tbsp (15ml)
- bacon - 1 cup (130g)

Preparation:

1. Cut the bacon.
2. Put all ingredients into the machine.
3. Set it to the Basic program.
4. Enjoy this tasty bread!

Nutritional facts:

Calories: 391, Fat: 9g, Carbs: 59g, Protein: 14g, Sugar: 4g, Potassium: 121mg, Sodium: 960mg

14.4 Sausage Bread

Preparation Time: 2 hours
Cook Time: 2 hours
Servings: 1 loaf (8 servings), 1.84 lb, 5 and 1/3 cups, 834.84 g

Ingredients:

- dry yeast - 1 1/2 tsp (6.84g)
- sugar- 1 tsp (5g)
- flour - 3 cups (360g)
- whey - 1 1/3 cup (340g)
- salt- 1 1/2 tsp (6.84g)
- chopped smoked sausage- 1 cup (130g)
- oil- 1 Tbsp (15ml)

Preparation:

1. Fold all the ingredients in the order that is recommended specifically for your model.
2. Set the required parameters for baking bread.
3. When ready, remove the delicious hot bread.
4. Wait until it cools down and enjoy sausage.

Nutritional facts:

Calories: 234, Fat: 5g, Carbs: 38g, Protein: 7g, Sugar: 2g, Potassium: 78mg, Sodium: 535mg

14.5 Cheese Sausage Bread

Preparation Time: 2 hours
Cook Time: 2 hours
Servings: 1 loaf (8 servings), 1.15 lb, 5 and 1/3 cups, 522 g

Ingredients:

- dry yeast - 1 tsp (5g)
- salt- 1 tsp (5g)
- flour - 3 ½ cup (438g)
- oil - 1 ½ tbsp (22ml)
- sugar - 1 Tbsp (15g)
- grated cheese - 2 Tbsp (30g)
- smoked sausage- 2 Tbsp (30g)
- water - 1 cup (130ml)
- chopped garlic- 1 Tbsp (15g)

Preparation:

1. Cut the sausage into small cubes.
2. Grate the cheese on a grater
3. Chop the garlic.
4. Add all ingredients to the machine according to the instructions.
5. Turn on the baking program and let it do the work.

Nutritional facts:

Calories: 260, Fat: 5g, Carbs: 43g, Protein: 7g, Sugar: 1.7g, Potassium: 112mg, Sodium: 334mg

14.6 Collards & Bacon Loaf

Preparation Time: 15 minutes
Cook Time: 15 minutes
Servings: 1 loaf (4 servings), 1.87 lb, 5 cups, 850g

Ingredients:

- whole-wheat pizza dough- 1 lb (453g)
- thinly sliced cooked collard greens - 2 cups (240g)
- garlic-flavored olive oil - 3 Tbsp (42ml)
- crumbled cooked bacon- ¼ cups (59g)
- shredded Cheddar cheese- 1 cup (130g)

Preparation:

1. Heat grill to medium-high.
2. Roll out dough to an oval that's 12 inches on a surface that's lightly floured. Move to a big baking sheet that's lightly floured. Put Cheddar, collards, oil, and dough on the grill.
3. Grease grill rack. Move to grill the crust. Cover the lid and cook for 1-2 minutes until it becomes light brown and puffed.
4. Use tongs to flip over the crust—spread oil on the crust and top with Cheddar and collards. Close lid and cook until cheese melts for another 2-3 minutes or the crust is light brown at the bottom.
5. Put pizza on the baking sheet and top using bacon.

Nutritional facts: Calories: 498, Fat: 28g, Carbs: 50g, Protein: 19g, Sugar: 3g, Potassium: 122mg, Sodium: 573mg

15 SOURDOUGH BREADS

15.1 Honey Sourdough Bread

Preparation Time: 15 minutes
Cook Time: 3 hours
Servings: 1 loaf, 1.21 lb, 4 5/6 cups (4 cups and 6 2/3 tbsp), 719.84 g

Ingredients:

- sourdough starter- 2/3 cup (227g)
- vegetable oil - 1 Tbsp (15ml)
- water - ½ cup (125ml)
- salt- 1/2 tsp (2.84g)
- honey - 2 Tbsp (30ml)
- bread flour- 2 cups (240g)
- high protein wheat flour - ½ cup (100g)
- active dry yeast - 1 tsp (5g)

Preparation:

1. Measure 1 cup (130g) of starter and add the residual bread ingredients to the bread machine pan.
2. Choose the basic/white bread cycle with medium or light crust color.

Nutritional facts: Calories: 175, Fat: 0.3g, Carbs: 33g, Protein: 5.6g, Sugar: 1g, Potassium: 97mg, Sodium: 121mg

15.2 Multigrain Sourdough Bread

Preparation Time: 15 minutes
Cook Time: 3 hours
Servings: 1 loaf, 2.09 lb, 8 1/4 cups (8 cups and 1 tbsp), 948 g

Ingredients:

- sourdough starter- 2 cups (240g)
- milk - ½ cup (118ml)
- butter, 2 Tbsp (30g)or 2 Tbsp (30ml)olive oil
- honey - ¼ cups (59ml)
- salt - 1 tsp (5g)
- millet, ½ cup (100g) or ½ cup (100g) amaranth or ½ cup (100g) quinoa
- sunflower seeds - ½ cup (100g)
- multi-grain flour - 3 ½ cup (438g)

Preparation:

1. Add ingredients to the bread machine pan.
2. Choose the dough cycle.
3. When the cycle is over, take out dough and place on a lightly floured surface, and shape it into a loaf.
4. Put in a greased loaf pan, cover, and rise until the bread is a couple of inches above the edge.
5. For 40 to 50 minutes, bake at 375°F.

Nutritional facts: Calories: 110, Fat: 1.8g, Carbs: 13g, Protein: 2.7g, Sugar: 1g, Potassium: 76mg, Sodium: 213mg

15.3 Olive and Garlic Sourdough Bread

Preparation Time: 15 minutes; 1 week (starter)
Cook Time: 3 hours
Servings: Serving: 1 loaf, 1.69 lb, 6 2/3 cups (6 cups and 2 2/3 tbsp), 768.4 g

Ingredients:

- sourdough starter- 2 cups (240g)
- olive oil - 2 Tbsp (30ml)
- flour- 3 cups (360g)
- salt - 2 tsp (8.4g)
- sugar - 2 Tbsp (30g)
- chopped garlic - 6 cloves
- chopped black olives- ½ cup (100g)

Preparation:

1. Add the starter and bread ingredients to the bread machine pan.
2. Choose the dough cycle.
3. Preheat oven to 375°F(190 degrees C).
4. When the cycle is complete, if the dough is sticky, add more flour.
5. Shape dough onto a baking sheet or put into a loaf pan
6. Bake for 35-45 minutes until golden.
7. Cool before slicing.

Nutritional facts:

Calories: 150, Fat: 0.5g, Carbs: 26.5g, Protein: 3.4g, Sugar: 1g, Potassium: 78mg, Sodium: 267mg

15.4 Sourdough Boule

Preparation Time: 4 hours
Cook Time: 25-35 minutes
Servings: 1 large boule or 12 servings, 2.84 lb, 10 7/8 cups (10 cups and 7 tbsp), 1290 g

Ingredients:

- warm water- 1 1/8 cup (275 ml)
- all-purpose flour- 4 cups (550 g)
- sourdough starter - 4 cups (500 g)
- salt- 1 ½ tbsp (20 g)

Preparation:

1. Combine the flour, warm water, and starter, and let it sit, covered for at least 30 minutes.
2. After letting it sit, stir in the salt, and turn dough out onto a surface dusted with flour. It should be sticky; you do not have to worry.
3. Flatten the dough slightly (it's best to "slap" it onto the counter), then fold it in half a few times.
4. Cover the dough and let it rise. Repeat the slap and fold a few more times. Now cover the dough and let it rise for 2-4 hours.
5. When the dough is at least doubles in size, gently pull it, so the top of the dough is exposed. Repeat several times. Let it rise for 2-4 hours once more.
6. Preheat to oven to 475°F (246 degrees C), and either place a baking stone or a cast iron pan in the oven to preheat.
7. Place the risen dough on the stone or pot, and score the top in several spots. For 20 minutes, bake, then reduce the heat to 475°F (246 degrees C), and bake for 25-35 minutes more. The boule will be golden brown.

Nutritional facts:

Calories: 243, Fat: 0.7g, Carbs: 4g, Protein: 6.9g, Sugar: 1g, Potassium: 89mg, Sodium: 392mg

15.5 Herbed Baguette

Preparation Time: 45 minutes

Cook Time: 20-25 minutes

Servings: 3 baguettes, 3.72 lb, 13 3/4 cups (13 cups and 3 tbsp), 1690.84 g

Ingredients:

- warm water - 1 ¼ cups (178ml)
- sourdough starter, either fed or unfed- 2 cups (240g)
- all-purpose flour- 4 to 5 cups (946g to 1182g)
- salt- 2 1/2 tsp (10.84g)
- sugar - 2 tsp (8.4g)
- instant yeast - 1 Tbsp (15g)
- fresh oregano, chopped- 1 Tbsp (15g)
- fresh rosemary, chopped- 1 tsp (5g)
- fresh basil, chopped- 1 Tbsp (15g)
- Any other desired herbs

Preparation:

1. In the bowl of a mixer, combine all the ingredients, knead with a dough hook (or use your hands) until a smooth dough is formed—about 7 to 10 minutes; if necessary, add more flour.
2. Oil a bowl and place the dough, cover, and let it rest for about 2 hours.
3. Beat the dough and divide it into 3 parts. Create each piece of dough into a loaf of bread, about 16 inches long. You can do this by rolling the dough into a trunk, folding it, rolling it into a trunk, and then folding it again.
4. Place the rolled baguette dough onto lined baking sheets, and cover. Let it rise for one hour.
5. Preheat oven to 475°F (246 degrees C), and bake for 20-25 minutes

Nutritional facts:

Calories: 197, Fat: 0.6g, Carbs: 4g, Protein: 5g, Sugar: 1g, Potassium: 67mg, Sodium: 212mg

15.6 Czech Sourdough Bread

Preparation Time: 15 minutes

Cook Time: 3 hours

Servings: 1 loaf, 2.2 lb, 8 1/3 cups (8 cups and 1 1/3 tbsp), 998.4 g

Ingredients:

- non-dairy milk- 1 cup (175ml)
- honey - 1 Tbsp (15ml)
- salt - 1 Tbsp (15g)
- rye flour - 1 ½ cup (188g)
- sourdough starter - 1 cup (130g)
- wheat flour- ¾ cup (150g)
- bread flour - 1 cup (130g)
- wheat gluten- 5 Tbsp (70g)
- grated half-baked potato - 1 ½ cup (200g)
- caraway seeds - 2 tsp (8.4g)

Preparation:

1. Fill the bread machine pan with the ingredients.
2. Decide on the dough cycle.
3. The dough should rise in the bread machine for up to 24 hours until it doubles in size. Bake in the bread machine for an hour after rising.

Nutritional facts: Calories: 132, Fat: 0.8g, Carbs: 4g, Protein: 6.5g, Sugar: 1g, Potassium: 89mg, Sodium: 888mg

15.7 Sauerkraut Rye

Preparation Time: 2 hours 20 minutes
Cook Time: 50 minutes
Servings: 1 loaf, 1.72 lb, 6 1/3 cups (6 cups and 1 1/3 tbsp), 781.8 g

Ingredients:

- sauerkraut, rinsed and drained- 1 cup (130g)
- molasses- 1½ tbsp (22g)
- warm water - ¾ cup (150ml)
- brown sugar- 1½ tbsp (22g)
- butter- 1½ tbsp (22g)
- salt – 1 1/2 tsp (8.4g)
- caraway seeds- 1 tsp (5g)
- bread flour- 2 cups (240g)
- rye flour- 1 cup (130g)
- active dry yeast- 1 1/2 tsp (8.4g)

Preparation:

1. Put all the ingredients to your bread machine.
2. Set the program of your bread machine to Basic/White Bread and set crust type to Medium.
3. Wait until the cycle completes.
4. Once the loaf is ready, take the bucket out and allow bread to cool for 5 minutes.
5. Lightly shake the bucket to take out the loaf.

Nutritional facts: Calories: 75, Fat: 2g, Carbs: 13g, Protein: 2g, Sugar: 1g, Potassium: 27mg, Sodium: 192mg

15.8 French Sourdough Bread

Preparation Time: 15 minutes
Cook Time: 3 hours
Servings: 2 loaves, 3.47 lb, 9 1/3 cups (9 cups and 1 1/3 tbsp), 1574 g

Ingredients:

- sourdough starter- 2 cups (240g)
- water- ½ cup (125ml)
- salt - 1 tsp (5g)
- white cornmeal - 2 Tbsp (30g)
- white bread flour - 4 cups (544g)

Preparation:

1. Put the ingredients in the bread machine pan, saving cornmeal for later.
2. Choose the dough cycle.
3. Preheat oven to 375°F (190 degrees C).
4. At the end of the dough cycle, place dough onto a surface that is floured.
5. Add flour if the dough is sticky.
6. Divide dough into 2 portions and flatten it into an oval shape 1½ inch thick.
7. Fold ovals in half lengthwise and pinch seams to elongate.
8. Sprinkle cornmeal onto the baking sheet and place the loaves seam side down.
9. Cover and let it rise in until is about in doubled.
10. Place a deep pan of hot water on the bottom shelf of the oven
11. Use a knife to make shallow, diagonal slashes in the top of the loaves
12. Place the loaves in the oven and sprinkle with fine water. Spray the oven walls as well.
13. Repeat spraying 3 times at one-minute intervals.
14. Remove the pan of water after 15 minutes of baking
15. Fully bake for 30 to 40 minutes or till golden brown.

Nutritional facts: Calories: 937, Fat: 0.4g, Carbs: 196g, Protein: 26g, Sugar: 1g, Potassium: 178mg, Sodium: 1172mg

16 FRUIT BREAD

16.1 Banana Bread

Preparation Time: 1 hour 40 minutes
Cook Time: 1 loaf, 1.04 lb, 3 3/4 cups, 442.84g
Servings: 1 loaf

Ingredients:

- Baking powder- 1 tsp (5g)
- bananas, peeled and halved lengthwise – 2
- Baking soda- 1/2 tsp (2.84g)
- eggs- 2
- all-purpose flour- 2 cups (240g)
- white sugar - 3/4 cup (150g)
- Vegetable oil - 3 tbsp (45ml)

Preparation:

1. Put all the ingredients in the bread pan—select dough setting. Start and mix for about 3-5 minutes.
2. After 3-5 minutes, press stop. Do not continue to mix. Smooth out the top of the dough
3. Using the spatula and then select bake, start and bake for about 50 minutes. After 50 minutes, insert a toothpick into the top center to test doneness.
4. Test the loaf again. When the bread is completely baked, take out pan from the machine and let the bread remain in the pan for ten minutes. Take out bread and cool on a wire rack.

Nutritional facts: Calories: 310, Fat: 13g, Carbs: 40g, Protein: 6g, Sugar: 1g, Potassium: 120mg, Sodium: 564mg

16.2 Orange and Walnut Bread

Preparation Time: 2 hours 50 minutes
Cook Time: 45 minutes | **Servings:** 1 loaf (10-15 servings), 1.66 lb, 6 1/3 cups, 755g

Ingredients:

- egg white- 1
- warm whey- ½ cup (100g)
- water- 1 Tbsp (15ml)
- sugar- 4 tbsp (60g)
- yeast- 1 Tbsp (15g)
- flour- 4 cups (544g)
- oranges, crushed- 2
- salt - 1 ½ tbsp (20g)
- salt- 1 tsp (5g)
- vanilla - 1/3 tsp (15g)
- orange peel- Three tsp
- Crushed pepper, salt, cheese for garnish
- walnut and almonds, crushed- 3 Tbsp (42g)

Preparation:

1. Put all of the ingredients in your Bread Machine (except egg white, 1 Tbsp (15g) water, and crushed pepper/ cheese).
2. Set the program to the "Dough" cycle and let the cycle run.
3. Remove the dough (using lightly floured hands) and carefully place it on a surface dusted with flour.
4. Conceal with a light film/cling paper and let the dough rise for 10 minutes.
5. Divide the dough into thirds after it has risen
6. Place on a lightly flour surface, roll each portion into 14x10 inch sized rectangles
7. Use a sharp knife to cut carefully cut the dough into strips of ½ inch width
8. Pick 2-3 strips and twist them multiple times, making sure to press the ends together
9. Preheat your oven to 400 degrees F(204 degrees C).
10. Take a bowl and stir egg white, water, and brush onto the breadsticks

11. Sprinkle salt, pepper/ cheese
12. Bake for 10-12 minutes till golden brown
13. Take out from the baking sheet, then place on a cooling rack. Serve and enjoy!

Nutritional facts:

Calories: 437, Fat: 7g, Carbs: 82g, Protein: 12g, Sugar: 1g, Potassium: 27mg, Sodium: 678mg

16.3 Apple with Pumpkin Bread

Preparation Time: 2 hours 50 minutes
Cook Time: 45 minutes
Servings: 2 loaves, 2.33 lb per loaf, 8 3/4 cups per loaf, 1056.28g per loaf

Ingredients:

- dried apples, chopped- 1/3 cup (113g)
- almond flour - 4 cups (544g)
- bread machine yeast- 1 1/2 tsp (8g)
- ground nutmeg- 1/4 tsp (1.42g)
- ground pecans- 1/3 cup (113g)
- allspice- 1/4 tsp (1.42g)
- ground ginger - 1/4 tsp (1.42g)
- salt - 1 1/4 tsp (1.42g)
- ground cinnamon- 1/2 tsp (2.84g)
- dry skim milk powder- 1/3 cup (113g)
- unsalted butter, cubed - 2 Tbsp (30g)
- large eggs, at room temperature- 2
- honey- 1/4 cup (21g)
- water, 2/3 cup (227g) with a temperature of 80 to 90 degrees F (26 to 32 degrees C)
- pumpkin puree- 2/3 cup (227g)

Preparation:

1. Put all ingredients, excluding the dried apples, in the bread pan in this order: water, pumpkin puree, eggs, honey, skim milk, butter, salt, allspice, cinnamon, pecans, nutmeg, ginger, flour, and yeast.
2. Secure the pan in the machine and lock the lid.
3. Place the dried apples in the fruit and nut dispenser.
4. Turn on the machine. Choose the sweet setting and your desired color of the crust.
5. Carefully take out the baked bread once ready and leave it to cool for 20 minutes before slicing.

Nutritional facts: Calories: 228, Fat: 4g, Carbs: 30g, Protein: 18g, Sugar: 1g, Potassium: 122mg, Sodium: 345mg

16.4 Date Delight Bread

Prep Time: 2 hours | **Cook Time:** 15 minutes
Servings: 1 loaf (12 servings), 1.48 lb,
5 1/3 cups, 672g

Ingredients:

- water, lukewarm- ¾ cup (177ml)
- butter, melted at room temperature - 2 Tbsp (30g)
- milk, lukewarm- ½ cup (125ml)
- molasses - 3 Tbsp (42g)
- honey - ¼ cups (59g)
- whole-wheat flour- 2 ¼ cups (340g)
- sugar- 1 Tbsp (15g)
- skim milk powder - 2 Tbsp (30g)
- white almond flour - One ¼ cups (59g)s
- salt- 1 tsp (5g)
- instant or bread machine yeast - 1 1/2 tsp (2.84g)
- unsweetened cocoa powder - 1 Tbsp (15g)
- chopped dates- ¾ cup (150g)

Preparation:

1. Take 1 ½ pound size loaf pan and add the liquid ingredients and then add the dry ingredients. (Do not add the dates as of now.)
2. Place the loaf pan in the machine and close its top lid.
3. Plug the bread machine into the power socket. For selecting a bread cycle, press "Basic Bread/White Bread/Regular Bread" or "Fruit/Nut Bread," and for choosing a crust type, press "Light" or "Medium."
4. Start the machine, and it will start preparing the bread. When the machine beeps or signals, add the dates.
5. After the bread loaf is completed, open the lid and take out the loaf pan.
6. Allow the pan to cool down for 10-15 minutes on a wire rack. Gently shake the pan and remove the bread loaf.
7. Make slices and serve.

Nutritional facts: Calories: 220, Fat: 5g, Carbs: 52g, Protein: 6g, Sugar: 1g, Potassium: 87mg, Sodium: 321mg

16.5 Sun Vegetable Bread

Preparation Time: 15 minutes
Cook Time: 3 hours 45 minutes
Servings: 1 loaf (8 slices), 1.27 lb, 4 1/2 cups, 576.4g

Ingredients:

- wheat flour - 2 cups (250 g)
- panifarin- 2 tsp (8.4g)
- whole-wheat flour - 2 cups (250 g)
- salt – 1 1/2 tsp (8.4g)
- yeast- 2 tsp (8.4g)
- paprika dried slices - 1 Tbsp (15g)
- sugar - 1 Tbsp (15g)
- dried garlic- 1 Tbsp (15g)
- dried beets- 2 Tbsp (30g)
- vegetable oil - 1 Tbsp (15ml)
- water- 1½ cup (188ml)

Preparation:

1. Set baking program, which should be 4 hours; crust color is Medium.
2. Be sure to look at the kneading phase of the dough to get a smooth and soft bun.

Nutritional facts:
Calories: 253, Fat: 2.6g, Carbs: 49g, Protein: 7g, Sugar: 1g, Potassium: 179mg, Sodium: 444mg

16.6 Tomato Onion Bread

Preparation Time: 10 minutes
Cook Time: 3 hours 50 minutes
Servings: 1 loaf (12 slices), 1.11 lb, 4 cups, 504.24g

Ingredients:

- all-purpose flour - 2 cups (240g)
- warm water - ½ cup (100ml)
- whole meal flour- 1 cup (130g)
- olive oil - 3 Tbsp (42ml)
- milk - 4 3/4 ounces (140 ml)
- salt- 1 tsp (5g)
- sugar - 2 Tbsp (30g)
- baking powder - 1/2 tsp (2.84g)
- dry yeast - 2 tsp (8.4g)
- onion- 1
- sun-dried tomatoes- 5
- black pepper- ¼ tsp (8.4g)

Preparation:

1. Prepare all the necessary products. Finely chop the onion and sauté in a frying pan. Cut up the sun-dried tomatoes (10 halves).
2. Pour all liquid ingredients into the bowl; then cover with flour and put in the tomatoes and onions. Pour in the yeast and baking powder without touching the liquid.
3. Select the baking cycle and start. You can choose the Bread with Additives program, and then the bread machine will knead the dough at low speeds.

Nutritional facts:

Calories: 241, Fat: 6g, Carbs: 40g, Protein: 6g, Sugar: 1g, Potassium: 45mg, Sodium: 305mg

16.7 Fragrant Orange Bread

Preparation Time: 5 Minutes
Cook Time: 25 Minutes
Servings: 1 loaf (8 servings), 1.24 lb, 4 1/2 cups, 562g

Ingredients:

- Milk- 1 cup (130ml)
- sugar- 3 Tbsp (42g)
- freshly clasped orange juice - 3 Tbsp (42ml)
- salt- 1 tsp (5g)
- melted butter cooled- 1 Tbsp (15g)
- Zest of 1 orange
- white almond flour- 3 cups (360g)
- bread machine or instant yeast - 1¼ tsp (7g)

Preparation:

1. Place the ingredients in your bread machine.
2. Select the Bake cycle. Select the light or medium crust option, set the machine to make white bread, and then click Start. When the loaf has finish baking, take the bucket out of the appliance. Allow the bread to cool for five minutes.
3. Moderately shake the pan to eliminate the loaf and put on a rack to cool.

Nutritional facts:

Calories: 277, Fat: 4g, Carbs: 48g, Protein: 9g, Sugar: 1g, Potassium: 87mg, Sodium: 321mg

16.8 Strawberry Shortcake Bread

Preparation Time: 10 Minutes
Cook Time: 25 Minutes
Servings: 1 loaf (8 servings), 1.21 lb, 4 1/4 cups, 549.4g

Ingredients:

- milk, 1/2 cup (125ml) at 80°F to 90°F (26 degree C to 32 degree C)
- sugar- 3 Tbsp (42g)
- melted butter, cooled- 3 Tbsp (42g)
- sliced fresh strawberries - ¾ cup (150g)
- salt – 1 1/2 tsp (8.4g)
- quick oats - 1 cup (130g)
- bread machine or instant yeast- 1 1/2 tsp (8.4g)
- white almond flour - 2¼ cups (281g)

Preparation:

1. Fill the bread machine with the ingredients.
2. Select the Bake cycle. Choose a light or medium crust, program the machine for Whitbread, and then press Start.
3. Remove the bucket from the device after the bread is done.
4. Give the bread five minutes to cool. Remove the loaf from the can with a little shake and place it on a cooling rack.

Nutritional facts:

Calories: 277, Fat: 6g, Carbs: 48g, Protein: 9g, Sugar: 1g, Potassium: 86mg, Sodium: 300mg

16.9 Pineapple Coconut Bread

Preparation Time: 15 Minutes
Cook Time: 1 Hour 10 Minutes
Servings: 1 loaf, 0.91 lb, 3 1/2 cups, 410g

Ingredients:

- coconut milk- ½ cup (125ml)
- coconut extract – 1 1/2 tsp (8.4g)
- shredded sweetened coconut - ¾ cup (75g)
- butter, at room temperature - 6 tbsp (90g)
- all-purpose flour - 2 cups (240g)
- sugar- 1 cup (200g)
- salt- 1/2 tsp (2.84g)
- eggs- 2
- baking powder- 1 tsp (5g)
- pineapple juice- ½ cup (120ml)

Preparation:

1. Preheat the oven to 350°F (175°C). Grease and flour a 9x5-inch loaf pan.
2. In a mixing bowl, combine the butter, eggs, coconut milk, pineapple juice, sugar, and coconut extract. Mix well.
3. In a separate bowl, whisk together the flour, shredded coconut, salt, and baking powder.
4. Gradually add the dry ingredients to the wet ingredients, mixing until just combined.
5. Pour the batter into the prepared loaf pan and smooth the top.
6. Bake for 1 hour to 1 hour 10 minutes, or until a toothpick inserted into the center comes out clean.
7. Remove from the oven and let the bread cool in the pan for 10 minutes. Then transfer to a wire rack to cool completely.

Nutritional facts: Calories: 256, Fat: 11g, Carbs: 36g, Protein: 3g, Sugar: 19g, Potassium: 103mg, Sodium: 192mg

16.10 Fruit Syrup Bread

Preparation Time: 10 Minutes
Cook Time: 25 Minutes
Servings: 1 loaf, 1.5 lb, 3 2/3 cups (or 3 cups and 10 tbsp), 464g

Ingredients:

- buckwheat flour - 3 2/3 cup (464g)
- unsalted butter, melted- 1/4 cup (21g)
- instant yeast- 1 1/2 tsp (2.84g)
- sugar - 2 Tbsp (30g)
- lukewarm water - 1 cup (125ml)
- rolled oats- 1/4 cup (21g)
- syrup from preserved fruit- 1/2 cup (100g)
- salt- 1/2 tsp (2.84g)

Preparation:

1. Combine the syrup and 1/2 cup (100ml) water. Heat until lukewarm. Add more water to precisely 1 cup (130ml) of water.
2. Place all the ingredients, except for the rolled oats and butter, in a liquid-dry-yeast layering.
3. Put the pan in the bread machine.
4. Load the rolled oats in the automatic dispenser.
5. Select the Bake cycle. Choose whole-wheat loaf.
6. Press start and wait until the loaf is cooked.
7. Brush the top with butter once cooked.
8. The machine will start the keep warm mode after the bread is complete.
9. Let it remain in that mode for about 10 minutes before unplugging.
10. Remove the pan and let it cool down for about 10 minutes.

Nutritional facts: Calories: 198, Fat: 6g, Carbs: 4g, Protein: 3g, Sugar: 1g, Potassium: 78mg, Sodium: 287mg

16.11 Lemon-Lime Blueberry Bread

Preparation Time: 10 Minutes
Cook Time: 25 Minutes
Servings: 1 loaf, 1.5 lb, 3 cups, 360g

Ingredients:

- plain yogurt at room temperature- 3/4 cup (150g)
- honey- 3 Tbsp (42g)
- water - 1/2 cup (125ml)
- salt - 1 1/2 tsp (8.4g)
- melted butter cooled - 1 Tbsp (15g)
- lime zest - 1 tsp (5g)
- lemon extract- 1/2 tsp (2.84g)
- white almond flour - 3 cups (360g)
- dried blueberries - 1 cup (130g)
- bread machine or instant yeast- 2¼ tsp (8.4g)

Preparation:

1. Fill the bread machine with the ingredients.
2. Selecting the Bake cycle. Choose a light or medium crust, program the machine for Whitbread, and then press Start.
3. Take the bucket out of the machine.
4. Give the bread five minutes to cool.
5. Remove the loaf from the pan with a little shake and place it on a cooling rack.

Nutritional facts: Calories: 222, Fat: 5g, Carbs: 4g, Protein: 6g, Sugar: 1g, Potassium: 27mg, Sodium: 321mg

16.12 Cranberry Yogurt Bread

Preparation Time: 10 Minutes
Cook Time: 25 Minutes
Servings: 1 loaf, 1.5 lb, 3 cups and 2 tbsp, 360g

Ingredients:

- bread or all-purpose flour- 3 cups (360g) + 2 Tbsp (30g)
- olive or coconut oil - 1 Tbsp (14ml)
- lukewarm water - 1/2 cup (125ml)
- sugar- 3 Tbsp (42g)
- orange or lemon essential oil- 1 Tbsp (15ml)
- instant yeast- 2 tsp (8.4g)
- yogurt- 3/4 cup (150g)
- raisins- 1/2 cup (100g)
- dried cried cranberries - 1 cup (130g)

Preparation:

1. Place all ingredients, except cranberries and raisins, in the bread pan in the liquid-dry-yeast layering.
2. Put the pan in the bread machine.
3. Load the fruits in the automatic dispenser.
4. Select the Bake cycle. Choose White bread.
5. Press start and wait until the loaf is cooked.
6. The machine will start the keep warm mode after the bread is complete.
7. Allow it to stay in that mode for at least 10 minutes before unplugging.
8. Remove the pan and let it cool down for about 10 minutes.

Nutritional facts:

Calories: 234, Fat: 4g, Carbs: 4g, Protein: 2g, Sugar: 1g, Potassium: 76mg, Sodium: 311mg

17 SWEET BREAD

17.1 Lemon Poppy Seed Bread

Preparation Time: 10 minutes
Cook Time: 4 hours
Servings: 1 loaf, 0.94 lb, 4 3/4 cups, 432g

Ingredients:

- Eggs- 3
- lemon juice- 1 1/2 Tbsp (45g)
- unsalted butter, melted- 1 1/2 Tbsp (45g)
- almond flour - 1 1/2 cup (240g)
- lemon, zested- 1
- baking powder- 1/4 tsp (1.42g)
- erythritol sweetener - 1/4 cup (21g)
- poppy seeds- 1 Tbsp (14g)

Preparation:

1. Beat eggs, butter, lemon juice, and lemon zest until combined.
2. Add flour, sweetener, baking powder, and poppy seeds in another bowl and mix well.
3. Add the egg mixture to the bread pan, top with the flour mixture, and cover.
4. Select the BASIC/WHITE cycle and click START.
5. Remove the bread when done. Cool, slice, and serve.

Nutritional facts:

Calories: 200, Fat: 15g, Carbs: 2g, Protein: 9g, Sugar: 1g, Potassium: 111mg, Sodium: 321mg

17.2 Cinnamon Sweet Bread

Preparation Time: 10 minutes
Cook Time: 1 hour
Servings: 1 loaf, 1.13 lb, 6 cups, 456g

Ingredients:

- cinnamon, ground - 3 tsp (15g)
- large eggs-3
- almond flour- 1 1/2 cup (240g)
- vanilla essence- 1 tsp (5g)
- keto sweetener- 1/2 cup (100g)
- sour cream- 1/4 cup (21g)
- coconut flour - 1/4 cup (21g)
- almond milk, unsweetened - 1/2 cup (100g)
- baking powder - 1 tsp (5g)
- unsalted butter, melted - 1/2 cup (100g)

Preparation:

1. Put all ingredients into the bread machine.
2. Close the lid and choose the sweet bread cycle.
3. When cooking is over, remove the bread from the machine and let it rest for about 10 minutes.

Nutritional facts:

Calories: 190, Fat: 15g, Carbs: 4.5g, Protein: 7g, Sugar: 1g, Potassium: 78mg, Sodium: 256mg

17.3 Basic Sweet Yeast Bread

Preparation Time: 3 hours
Cook Time: 20 minutes
Servings: 1 loaf, 1.25 lb, 8 cups, 544g

Ingredients:

- Egg- 1
- sugar - 1/3 cup (113g)
- butter - 1/4 cup (21g)
- salt - 1/2 tsp (2.84g)
- milk- 1 cup (130ml)
- active dry yeast- 1 Tbsp (14g)
- flour- 4 cups (544g)

After beeping:

- Fruits/groundnuts

Preparation:

1. Put all ingredients in the bread machine, carefully following the instructions of the manufacturer (except fruits/groundnuts).
2. Set the program of the bread machine to basic/sweet and set the crust type to light or medium.
3. Press start. Once the machine beeps, add fruits/ground nuts.
4. When the cycle is completed, take the bucket out and allow bread cool for 5 minutes.
5. Shake the bucket gently to take out the loaf, then transfer to a cooling rack, slice, and serve.

Nutritional facts:

Calories: 336, Fat: 7g, Carbs: 2g, Protein: 9g, Sugar: 1g, Potassium: 123mg, Sodium: 456mg

17.4 Apricot Prune Bread

Preparation Time: 3 hours
Cook Time: 20 minutes
Servings: 1 loaf, 1.25 lb, 8 cups, 544g

Ingredients:

- Egg- 1
- apricot juice- 1/4 cup (21g)
- whole milk - 4/5 cup (200ml)
- sugar - 1/5 cup (282g)
- butter - 1/4 cup (21g)
- instant yeast- 1 Tbsp (14g)
- prunes, chopped - 5/8 cup (125g)
- salt- 1/4 tsp (1.42g)
- dried apricots, chopped - 5/8 cup (125g)

Preparation:

1. Put all ingredients into the bread machine, carefully following the manufacturer's instructions (except apricots and prunes).
2. Set the program of the bread machine to basic/sweet and set the crust type to light or medium.
3. Press start. Once the machine beeps, add apricots and prunes.
4. When the cycle is completed, take the bucket out and allow bread to cool for 5 minutes.
5. Shake the bucket gently to take out loaf, then transfer to a cooling rack, slice, and serve.

Nutritional facts:

Calories: 362, Fat: 6g, Carbs: 2g, Protein: 11g, Sugar: 1g, Potassium: 122mg, Sodium: 467mg

17.5 Citrus Bread

Preparation Time: 3 hours
Cook Time: 1 hour
Servings: 1 loaf, 1.25 lb, 8 cups, 544g
Ingredients:

- Egg- 1
- sugar - 1/3 cup (113g)
- butter - 3 Tbsp (42g).
- orange juice - 1/2 cup (125ml)
- vanilla sugar - 1 Tbsp (14g)
- salt - 1 tsp (5g)
- milk- 2/3 cup (227ml)
- instant yeast- 1 Tbsp (14g)
- almond flour- 4 cup
- lemon, candied - 1/4 cup (21g)
- oranges, candied- 1/4 cup (21g)
- Almonds, Chopped - 1/4 cup (21g)
- lemon zest - 2 tsp (8.4g)

Preparation:

1. Add the ingredients to the breadmaker, paying close attention to the manufacturer's instructions (except candied fruits, zest, and almonds).
2. Set the program of the bread machine to basic/sweet and set the crust type to light or medium.
3. Press start. Once the machine beeps, add candied fruits, lemon zest, and chopped almonds.
4. When the cycle is completed, take the bucket out and allow bread to cool for 5 minutes.
5. After removing the bread from the bucket with a light shake, place it on a cooling rack, slice it, and serve.

Nutritional facts:

Calories: 402, Fat: 7g, Carbs: 3g, Protein: 12g, Sugar: 1g, Potassium: 167mg, Sodium: 578mg

17.6 Fruit Bread

Preparation Time: 3 hours
Cook Time: 40 minutes
Servings: 1 loaf, 1.25 lb, 8 cups, 544g
Ingredients:

- Egg- 1
- Rum- 2 Tbsp (30g)
- Milk- 1 cup (130ml)
- brown sugar- 1/4 cup (21g)
- butter - 1/4 cup (21g)
- instant yeast - 1 Tbsp (14g)
- almond flour- 4 cups (544g)
- salt - 1 tsp (5g)

Fruits:

- dried apricots, coarsely chopped- 1/4 cup (21g)
- candied cherry, pitted- 1/4 cup (21g)
- prunes, coarsely chopped- 1/4 cup (21g)
- almonds, chopped- 1/4 cup (21g)
- seedless raisins- 1/2 cup (100g)

Preparation:

1. Put all ingredients in the bread machine, carefully following the instructions of the manufacturer (except fruits).
2. Set the program of the bread machine to basic/sweet and set crust type to light or medium. Click start. Once the machine beeps, add fruits. When the cycle is completed, take the bucket out and allow bread to cool for 5 minutes.
3. Shake the bucket gently to take out the bread, then transfer to a cooling rack, slice, and serve.

Nutritional facts:

Calories: 440, Fat: 8g, Carbs: 3g, Protein: 12g, Sugar: 1g, Potassium: 113mg, Sodium: 594mg

17.7 Marzipan Cherry Bread

Preparation Time: 3 hours
Cook Time: 35 minutes
Servings: 1 loaf, 1.25 lb, 8 cups, 544g
Ingredients:

- Egg- 1
- almond liqueur - 1 Tbsp (14g)
- Milk- 3/4 cup (150ml)
- ground almonds- 1/2 cup (100g)
- orange juice- 4 tbsp (56ml)
- sugar- 1/3 cup (113g)
- butter - 1/4 cup (21g)
- instant yeast- 1 Tbsp (14g)
- almond flour- 4 cups (544g)
- marzipan- 1/2 cup (100g)
- salt- 1 tsp (5g)
- dried cherries, pitted- 1/2 cup (100g)

Preparation:

1. Put all ingredients into the bread machine, carefully following the instructions of the manufacturer (except marzipan and cherry).
2. Set the program of the bread machine to basic/sweet and set the crust type to light or medium.
3. Press start.
4. Once the machine beeps, add marzipan and cherry. When the cycle is completed, take the bucket out and allow bread cool for 5 minutes.
5. Shake the bucket gently to take out bread, then transfer to a cooling rack, slice, and serve.

Nutritional facts:

Calories: 508, Fat: 14g, Carbs: 3g, Protein: 18g, Sugar: 1g, Potassium: 127mg, Sodium: 692mg

17.8 Raspberry Bread

Preparation Time: 10 minutes
Cook Time: 50 minutes
Servings: 1 loaf, 0.94 lb, 4 3/4 cups, 432g
Ingredients:

- raspberries - 1 cup (130g)
- baking powder - 1 1/2 tsp (6.84g)
- sugar - 1/4 cup (21g)
- sour cream- 4 tbsp (56g)
- flour- 2 cups (240g)
- whole eggs- 2
- unsalted butter, melted- 4 tbsp (56g)
- lemon extract- 1 tsp (5g)
- vanilla- 1 tsp (5ml)
- lemon, juiced- 1/2

Preparation:

1. Put all the ingredients (except the raspberries) to the bread machine pan following the instructions for the device. Close the cover. Set the bread machine program to CAKE for 40–50 minutes.
2. After the signal, add the raspberries to the dough. Press START.
3. Check for doneness with a toothpick. The approximate baking time is 45 minutes.
4. Wait until the program is complete. When done, take the bucket out and let it cool for 10 minutes.
5. Shake the loaf from the pan and let it cool for 30 minutes on a cooling rack.
6. Slice and serve.

Nutritional facts:

Calories: 165, Fat: 12g, Carbs: 7g, Protein: 6g, Sugar: 1g, Potassium: 87mg, Sodium: 278mg

17.9 Blueberry Bread

Preparation Time: 10 minutes
Cook Time: 50 minutes
Servings: 1 loaf, 0.94 lb, 4 3/4 cups, 432g

Ingredients:

- Blueberries- 1/2 cup (100g)
- baking powder - 2 tsp (8.4g)
- sugar - 1/3 cup (113g)
- sour cream- 4 tbsp (56g)
- flour - 2 cups (240g)
- whole eggs-2
- unsalted butter, melted - 4 tbsp (56g)
- vanilla- 1 tsp (5ml)

Preparation:

1. In a large container, beat eggs with an electric mixer well.
2. Pour them into the bread machine pan. Add all other ingredients. Close the lid.
3. Set the bread machine program to CAKE for 45–60 minutes (depending on the device).
4. Press START. After the signal indicating the beginning of the BAKE cycle, add the blueberries.
5. After 35 minutes of baking, start checking for doneness using a toothpick. The approximate baking time is 45–50 minutes. Wait until the program is complete. When done, take the bucket out and let it cool for 10 minutes.
6. Shake the loaf from the pan and let it cool for 30 minutes on a cooling rack.
7. Slice and serve.

Nutritional facts:

Calories: 163, Fat: 11g, Carbs: 10g, Protein: 4g, Sugar: 6g, Potassium: 68mg, Sodium: 235mg

17.10 Avocado Bread

Prep Time: 10 min | **Cook Time:** 60–70 min
Servings: 1 loaf, 1.19 lb, 6 cups, 544g

Ingredients:

- avocados, mashed- 4
- coconut flour - 1 cup (130g)
- almond flour- 2 cups (240g)
- avocado oil- 5 Tbsp (70ml)
- monk fruit sweetener - 1/2 cup (100g)
- kosher salt - 1/2 tsp (2.84g)
- cocoa powder, unsweetened- 4 tbsp (56g)
- vanilla extract- 1 tsp (5g)
- baking soda- 1 tsp (5g)
- chocolate chips - 1 cup (130g)

Preparation:

1. In a large bowl, mix all of the dry ingredients.
2. In a blender, combine all of the wet ingredients.
3. Put the wet ingredients into the bread machine pan.
4. Cover them with dry ingredients. Add half of the chocolate chips.
5. Close the cover. Set the bread machine program to CAKE. The time may differ depending on the device.
6. Press START. Help the machine to knead the dough, if necessary.
7. Before baking, top the bread with the remaining 1/2 cup (100g) of chocolate chips.
8. After 45 minutes of baking, start checking for doneness using a toothpick. The approximate baking time is 45–60 minutes. Wait until the program is complete.
9. When done, take the bucket out and let it cool for 10 minutes.
10. Shake the loaf from the pan and let it cool for 30 minutes on a cooling rack.
11. Slice and serve.

Nutritional facts: Calories: 287, Fat: 22g, Carbs: 15g, Protein: 6g, Sugar: 3g, Potassium: 121mg, Sodium: 309mg

17.11 Gingerbread Cake

Prep Time: 10 min | **Cook Time:** 45 min
Servings: 1 loaf, 0.94 lb, 4 3/4 cups, 432g

Ingredients:

- large eggs- 4
- vanilla extract- 1 tsp (5g)
- butter, melted- 1/4 cup (21g)
- flour - 3/4 cup (150g)
- granulated sugar- 3/4 cup (150g)
- ginger, ground- 2 tsp (8.4g)
- baking powder- 1 tsp (5g)
- allspice, ground - 1/2 tsp (2.84g)
- cinnamon, ground- 2 tsp (8.4g)
- clove, ground- 1/2 tsp (2.84g)
- nutmeg, ground- 1/2 tsp (2.84g)
- kosher salt- 1/4 tsp (1.42g)

For the icing:

- vanilla extract - 1 tsp (5g)
- sugar- 1/4 cup (21g)
- walnuts, chopped- 1/4 cup (21g)
- cream cheese, softened- 1/2 cup (100g)

Preparation:

1. Whisk together the eggs, vanilla, and unsalted butter.
2. In a container, mix all the dry ingredients. Put the wet ingredients in the bread machine pan.
3. Cover them with dry ingredients. Close the lid.
4. Set the bread machine program to CAKE. The time may differ depending on the device.
5. Press START. After 30 minutes of baking, start checking for doneness using a toothpick. The approximate baking time is 40–45 minutes. Wait until the program is complete. When done, take the bucket out and let it cool for 10 minutes.
6. Shake the loaf from the pan and let it cool for 30 minutes on a cooling rack.
7. Slice and serve.

Nutritional facts: Calories: 138, Fat: 4g, Carbs: 4g, Protein: 5g, Sugar: 2g, Potassium: 99mg, Sodium: 289mg

17.12 Lemon Bread

Prep Time: 5 min | **Cook Time:** 1 hour
Servings: 1 loaf, 0.94 lb, 4 3/4 cups, 432g

Ingredients:

- flour - 9.5 oz. (269g)
- sugar- 1/2 cup (100g)
- baking powder- 1/2 tsp (2.84g)
- lemons zest – 2
- poppy seeds - 2 Tbsp (30g)
- butter, melted - 3 Tbsp (42g)
- lemon juice- 2 Tbsp (30ml)
- whole eggs - 6

For the Icing:

- sugar- 1/2 cup (100g)
- lemon juice - 1 Tbsp (14g)
- water- 2 Tbsp (30g)

Preparation:

1. Put all ingredients into the bread machine pan. Close the lid.
2. Set the bread machine program to CAKE. The time may differ depending on the device.
3. Press START. Help the machine to knead the dough, if necessary.
4. After 40 minutes of baking, start checking for doneness using a toothpick. The approximate baking time is 45–55 minutes.
5. Wait until the program is complete, and when done, take the bucket out and let it cool for 10 minutes.
6. Shake the loaf from the pan and let it cool for 30 minutes on a cooling rack.
7. Make the icing in a small bowl, mixing all the ingredients. Drizzle it over the bread.
8. Slice and serve.

Nutritional facts: Calories: 191, Fat: 15g, Carbs: 14g, Protein: 6g, Sugar: 5g, Potassium: 67mg, Sodium: 234mg

18 GLUTEN-FREE BREAD

18.1 Gluten-free Pumpkin Pie Bread

Prep Time: 5 min | **Cook Time:** 2 h 50 min | **Servings:** 1 loaf, 0.81 lb, 2.9 cups (and 2 tbsp if necessary), 370g

Ingredients:

- olive oil- 1/4 cup (59ml)
- bourbon vanilla extract- 1 Tbsp (15g)
- large eggs, beaten- 2
- honey - 4 tbsp (56g)
- canned pumpkin- 1 cup (130g)
- buckwheat flour - 1/2 cup (100g)
- lemon juice - 1/4 tsp (1.42g)
- sorghum flour - 1/4 cup (21g)
- millet flour- 1/4 cup (21g)
- light brown sugar- 1 cup (130g)
- tapioca starch - 1/2 cup (100g)
- baking soda - 1 tsp (5g)
- baking powder - 2 tsp (8.4g)
- xanthan gum - 1 tsp (5g)
- sea salt- 1/2 tsp (2.84g)
- allspice - 1 tsp (5g)
- ground cinnamon - 1 tsp (5g)
- peach juice- 1-2 Tbsp (30ml)

Preparation:

1. In a bowl, combine the dry ingredients and set them aside.
2. Add the moist ingredients to the pan, excluding the peach juice.
3. Fill the bread maker's pan with the dry ingredients.
4. Click Start after selecting the Sweet bread cycle and choosing a light or medium crust color.
5. As the ingredients begin to combine, scrape down the edges with a delicate silicone spatula.
6. If the batter is too stiff, add peach juice 1 Tbsp at a time until the batter is similar in consistency to muffin batter.
7. Put the lid on and bake the meal. Put on a cooling rack for 20 minutes before slicing.

Nutritional facts: Calories: 180, Fat: 5g, Carbs: 33g, Protein: 6g, Sugar: 5g, Potassium: 98mg, Sodium: 299mg

18.2 Gluten-free Pull-apart Rolls

Preparation Time: 5 minutes
Cook Time: 2 hours | **Servings:** 1 loaf, 1.57 lb, 2.75 cups (and 2 tbsp if necessary), 390g

Ingredients:

- warm water - 1 cup (130ml)
- Egg, room temperature- 1
- butter, unsalted - 2 Tbsp (30g)
- gluten-free almond-blend flour- 2 3/4 cup (390g)
- xanthan gum- 1 1/2 tsp (8.4g)
- apple cider vinegar - 1 tsp (5g)
- salt - 1 tsp (5g)
- Sugar- 1/4 cup (21g)
- active dry yeast- 2 tsp (8.4g)

Preparation:

1. Add the wet ingredients to the pan of the breadmaker.
2. Combine the dry ingredients in a pan, omitting the yeast.
3. Insert the yeast into the center of the dry ingredients.
4. Click Start after selecting the Dough cycle.
5. Spray nonstick cooking spray into an 8-inch round cake pan.
6. As soon as the dough cycle is over, split the dough into nine balls, place the balls in a cake pan, and thoroughly moisten the balls with warm water.
7. Put the ingredients in a warm place and cover with a cloth to allow it rise for an hour.
8. Set the oven to 400°F (204 degrees c).
9. Bake for 26 to 28 minutes, or until the top is golden.
10. Serve after brushing with butter.

Nutritional facts: Calories: 568, Fat: 10g, Carbs: 46g, Protein: 6g, Sugar: 1g, Potassium: 156mg, Sodium: 657mg

18.3 Gluten-free Whole Grain Bread

PrepTime: 5 min | **Cook Time:** 3 h 40 min | **Servings:** 1 loaf, 1.96 lb, 3.16 cups (and 3 tbsp if necessary), 562g

Ingredients:

- sorghum flour- 2/3 cup (227g)
- millet flour - 1/2 cup (100g)
- buckwheat flour- 1/2 cup (100g)
- xanthan gum- 2 1/4 tsp (1.42g)
- potato starch- 3/4 cup (150g)
- skim milk- 3/4 cup (150g)
- salt - 1 1/4 tsp (1.42g)
- instant yeast - 1 Tbsp (15g)
- Water- 1/2 cup (125ml)
- large egg, lightly beaten- 1
- agave nectar, separated - 5 tsp (25ml)
- extra virgin olive oil - 4 tbsp (56g)
- poppy seeds- 1 Tbsp (15g)
- cider vinegar - 1/2 tsp (2.84g)

Preparation:

1. Combine the potato starch, xanthan gum, sea salt, sorghum, buckwheat, and millet in a bowl.
2. In a measuring cup made of glass, mix the milk and water. Between 110°F and 120°F should be reached before adding the yeast and 2 tsp (8.4g) of agave nectar. For a few minutes, cover and set aside.
3. Combine the yeast and milk mixture with the olive oil, vinegar, last of the agave, and egg in a new mixing dish. Put wet ingredients in the bottom of the breadmaker.
4. Add the dry ingredients on top.
5. Press Start after selecting the gluten-free cycle and light colored crust.

6. Poppy seeds should be sprinkled after the second kneading cycle.
7. Pan from bread machine removed. After about 5 minutes, remove the loaf from the pan and let it cool on a rack.
8. Enjoy!

Nutritional facts: Calories: 153, Fat: 5g, Carbs: 24g, Protein: 3g, Sugar: 1g, Potassium: 98mg, Sodium: 292mg

18.4 Gluten-free Cinnamon Raisin Bread

Preparation Time: 5 minutes
Cook Time: 3 hours | **Servings:** 1 loaf, 1.96 lb, 2.85 cups (and 1 tbsp if necessary), 562g

Ingredients:

- almond milk- 3/4 cup (150ml)
- warm water- 6 tbsp (90ml)
- flax meal - 2 Tbsp (30g)
- butter - 2 Tbsp (30g)
- apple cider vinegar- 1 1/2 tsp (8.4g)
- brown rice flour- 1 2/3 cup (227g)s
- honey - 1 1/2 Tbsp (45g)
- potato starch- 2 Tbsp (30g)
- corn starch - 1/4 cup (21g)
- cinnamon - 1 Tbsp (15g)
- xanthan gum - 1 1/2 tsp (8.4g)
- active dry yeast - 1 tsp (5g)
- salt - 1/2 tsp (2.84g)
- raisins - 1/2 cup (100g)

Preparation:

1. Flax and water are combined, then leave to stand for five minutes.
2. In another bowl, combine the dry ingredients; leave out the yeast.
3. Fill the bread machine with the wet ingredients.
4. After creating a hole in the middle, add the dry ingredients on top.
5. Add yeast to the well.
6. Select Light Crust Color, Gluten Free, and click Start.
7. Add raisins after the initial rising and kneading cycle.
8. After baking, remove from the oven and place on a cooling rack.

Nutritional facts:

Calories: 192, Fat: 4g, Carbs: 38g, Protein: 2.7g, Sugar: 3g, Potassium: 76mg, Sodium: 289mg

18.5 Gluten-free Pizza Crust

Preparation Time: 5 minutes
Cook Time: 2 hours | **Servings:** 1 loaf, 2.94 lb, 3.5 cups, 1330g

Ingredients:

- xanthan gum - 3 tsp (15g)
- potato starch- 1/2 cup (100g)
- cornstarch, 1 cup (130g) and extra for dusting
- Yeast- 2 Tbsp (30g)
- rice flour- 2 cups (240g)
- Milk- 1 cup (130ml)
- Water- 1/2 cup (125ml)
- olive oil - 1/2 cup (125ml)
- Sugar- 1/2 cup (100g)
- large eggs, room temperature - 3
- salt - 1 tsp (5g)

Preparation:

1. Pour the wet ingredients, which have been combined in a different container, into the bread machine pan.
2. Add the dry ingredients to the pan after combining all but the yeast.
3. The middle of the dry ingredients should include the yeast.
4. Select the Dough cycle, then hit Start.
5. Once the dough is prepared, form it into a pizza by pressing it out onto a surface that has been lightly dusted with corn starch. Use this dough with your preferred pizza recipe and toppings!

Nutritional facts: Calories: 463, Fat: 8g, Carbs: 79g, Protein: 7g, Sugar: 6g, Potassium: 134mg, Sodium: 689mg

18.6 Gluten-free Brown Bread

PrepTime: 5 minutes | **Cook Time:** 3 hours | **Servings:** 1 loaf, 2.62 lb, 3.68 cups, 1270g

Ingredients:

- large eggs, lightly beaten- 2
- canola oil- 3 Tbsp (42g)
- warm water - 1 3/4 cup (230g)
- oat flour - 3/4 cup (150g)
- brown rice flour - 1 cup (130g)
- potato starch- 1 1/4 cup (260g)
- tapioca starch - 1/4 cup (21g)
- brown sugar- 2 Tbsp (30g)
- Salt- 1 1/2 tsp (6.4g)
- nonfat dry milk powder- 1/2 cup (100g)
- gluten-free flaxseed meal - 2 Tbsp (30g)
- psyllium, whole husks - 3 Tbsp (42g)
- xanthan gum - 2 1/2 tsp (8.4g)
- gluten-free yeast for bread machines- 2 1/2 tsp (8.4g)

Preparation:

1. The bread machine pan should contain the eggs, water, and canola oil. Stir everything together.
2. In a sizable mixing basin, combine all of the dry ingredients with the exception of the yeast.
3. Over the wet components, layer the dry ingredients.
4. The yeast should be placed in the center of the dry ingredients.
5. Press Start after setting the gluten-free cycle and medium crust color.
6. Lay the pan on its side to cool when the bread has finished baking before slicing it to serve.

Nutritional facts: Calories: 201, Fat: 5g, Carbs: 35g, Protein: 5g, Sugar: 4g, Potassium: 99mg, Sodium: 390mg

18.7 Sorghum Bread Recipe

Preparation Time: 5 minutes
Cook Time: 3 hours |
Servings: 1 loaf, 2.49 lb, 3.63 cups, 870g

Ingredients:

- salt - 1/2 tsp (2.84g)
- Sugar- 3 Tbsp (42g)
- xanthan gum - 1 tsp (5g)
- guar gum - 1 tsp (5g)
- tapioca starch - 1 cup (130g)
- brown or white sweet rice flour- 1/2 cup (100g)
- sorghum flour - 1 1/2 cup (340g)
- eggs (room temperature, lightly beaten) – 3
- instant yeast - 2 1/4 tsp (1.42g)
- Vinegar- 1 1/2 tsp (6.4g)
- oil - 1/4 cup (21g)
- Warm milk - ¾ -1 cup (177ml-130ml)

Preparation:

1. In a mixing bowl, combine all of the dry ingredients excluding the yeast.
2. In the bread machine pan, layer the dry ingredients on top of the wet ingredients.
3. The yeast should be placed in the center of the dry ingredients.
4. Light crust color, Basic bread cycle selected, and Start button.
5. Before serving, take it out and place it on a wire rack to cool on its side.

Nutritional facts:

Calories: 169, Fat: 6g, Carbs: 25g, Protein: 3g, Sugar: 4g, Potassium: 67mg, Sodium: 151mg

18.8 Gluten-free Simple Sandwich Bread

Preparation Time: 5 minutes
Cook Time: 1 hour |
Servings: 1 loaf, 2.68 lb, 3.75 cups, 638g

Ingredients:

- sorghum flour- 1 1/2 cup (340g)
- gluten-free millet flour or gluten-free oat flour - 1/2 cup (100g)
- tapioca starch or potato starch (not potato flour!)- 1 cup (130g)
- fine sea salt- 1 1/4 tsp (1.42g)
- xanthan gum - 2 tsp (8.4g)
- warm water - 1 1/4 cup (260ml)
- gluten-free yeast for bread machines - 2 1/2 tsp (8.4g)
- honey or raw agave nectar - 1 Tbsp (15g)
- extra virgin olive oil - 3 Tbsp (42g)
- organic free-range eggs, beaten- 2
- mild rice vinegar or lemon juice - 1/2 tsp (2.84ml)

Preparation:

1. Whisk together all of the dry ingredients in a basin, excluding the yeast.
2. Pour the liquid ingredients into the bread machine pan first, then carefully pour the combined dry ingredients on top of the liquid.
3. The middle of the dry ingredients should include the yeast.
4. Click Start after choosing Rapid, 1 hour and 20 minutes, and a medium crust color.
5. Leave to cool for 15 minutes before slicing.

Nutritional facts: Calories: 137, Fat: 4g, Carbs: 22g, Protein: 2g, Sugar: 3g, Potassium: 49mg, Sodium: 85mg

18.9 Gluten-free Crusty Boule Bread

Preparation Time: 5 minutes
Cook Time: 3 hours |
Servings: 1 loaf, 3.61 lb, 4.25 cups, 1640g

Ingredients:

- gluten-free flour mix- 3 1/4 cup (400g)
- kosher salt - 1 1/2 tsp (6.4g)
- active dry yeast- 1 Tbsp (15g)
- warm water - 1 1/3 cup (333ml)
- guar gum - 1 Tbsp (15g)
- olive oil - 2 Tbsp (30ml) , plus 2 tsp (8ml)
- large eggs, room temperature- 2
- Honey- 1 Tbsp (15g)

Preparation:

1. In a sizable mixing bowl, combine all of the dry ingredients with the exception of the yeast; set aside.
2. In another mixing dish, stir the water, eggs, oil, and honey together.
3. Fill the bread machine with the wet ingredients.
4. Over the wet components, layer the dry ingredients.
5. The yeast should be placed in the center of the dry ingredients.
6. Press Start after selecting the Gluten-Free setting.
7. Take the baked bread out and let it totally cool. To use as a boule, hollow it out and fill it with soup or dip; then, slice it to serve.

Nutritional facts:

Calories: 480, Fat: 3g, Carbs: 78g, Protein: 2g, Sugar: 7g, Potassium: 27mg, Sodium: 356mg

18.10 Gluten-Free Raisin Bread

Prep Time: 5 min | **Cook Time:** 1 hour |
Servings: 1 loaf, 1.59 lb, 3.23 cups, 724g

Ingredients:

- warm water - 300ml (1 ¼ cups)
- honey - 2 Tbsp (30g)
- olive oil - 60ml (¼ cups)
- apple cider vinegar - 1 Tbsp (15g)
- egg whites - 2
- dry active yeast- 7g (2 tsp)
- granulated sugar- 2 Tbsp (30g)
- baking powder - 1/2 tsp (2.84g)
- gluten-free almond flour / or any other gluten-free flour, levelled - 200g (2 cups)
- Xanthan Gum - 2 tsp (8.4g)
- Tapioca/potato starch, levelled - 100g (1 cup)
- ground cinnamon - 1 tsp (5g)
- salt - 1 tsp (5g)
- raisins - 150g (1 cup)

Preparation:

1. According to your bread machine manufacturer, place all the ingredients into the bread machine's greased pan except raisins.
2. Select basic cycle / standard cycle/bake / quick bread / sweet bread setting
3. then choose crust color either medium or Light and press start to bake bread.
4. In the last kneading cycle, check the dough
5. it should be wet but thick, not like traditional bread dough. If the dough is too wet, put more flour, 1 Tbsp at a time, or until dough slightly firm.
6. Five minutes before the dough-kneading cycle is over, add the raisins.
7. Remove the baked bread from the pan and let it cool on a wire rack after the cycle is complete and the machine has shut off.

Nutritional facts: Calories: 89, Fat: 1g, Carbs: 12g, Protein: 6g, Sugar: 1g, Potassium: 27mg, Sodium: 10mg

18.11 Gluten-free Sourdough Bread

Preparation Time: 5 minutes
Cook Time: 3 hours |
Servings: 1 loaf, 2.52 lb, 3.52 cups, 840g

Ingredients:

- Water- 1 cup (100ml)
- ricotta cheese- 3/4 cup (150g)
- eggs - 3
- vegetable oil- 1/4 cup (21g)
- honey - 1/4 cup (21g)
- gluten-free sourdough starter- 3/4 cup (150g)
- cider vinegar - 1 tsp (5g)
- potato starch - 2/3 cup (227g)
- white rice flour - 2 cups (240g)
- dry milk powder - 1/2 cup (100g)
- tapioca flour - 1/3 cup (113g)
- salt - 1 1/2 tsp (6.4g)
- xanthan gum - 3 1/2 tsp (12.4g)

Preparation:

1. Pour the wet ingredients into the bread machine pan after mixing them.
2. Combine the dry ingredients in a sizable mixing bowl, and then pour the mixture over the wet components.
3. Select the Gluten-Free cycle and press Start.
4. After removing the pan from the oven, give the bread within around 10 minutes to cool.
5. Before slicing, transfer to a cooling rack.

Nutritional facts:

Calories: 299, Fat: 7g, Carbs: 46g, Protein: 5g, Sugar: 4g, Potassium: 79mg, Sodium: 327mg

18.12 Grain-free Chia Bread

Preparation Time: 5 minutes
Cook Time: 3 hours

Servings: 1 loaf, 2.47 lb, 4.11 cups, 972g
Ingredients:

- warm water - 1 cup (100ml)
- olive oil- 1/4 cup (21g)
- large organic eggs, room temperature- 3
- gluten-free chia seeds, ground to flour - 1 cup (130g)
- apple cider vinegar- 1 Tbsp (15g)
- potato starch- 1/2 cup (100g)
- almond meal flour - 1 cup (130g)
- millet flour - 3/4 cup (150g)
- coconut flour - 1/4 cup (21g)
- salt - 1 1/2 tsp (6.4g)
- xanthan gum- 1 Tbsp (15g)
- nonfat dry milk- 3 Tbsp (42g)
- sugar - 2 Tbsp (30g)
- instant yeast- 6 tsp

Preparation:

1. Add the wet ingredients to the bread machine pan after whisking them together.
2. Add the dry ingredients, minus the yeast, to the wet ingredients after whisking them together.
3. Add yeast after making a hole in the dry ingredients.
4. Press Start after selecting the Whole Wheat cycle and light crust color.
5. Prior to serving, let the bread totally cool.

Nutritional facts:

Calories: 375, Fat: 18g, Carbs: 42g, Protein: 12g, Sugar: 6g, Potassium: 78mg, Sodium: 462mg

18.13 Easy Gluten-free, Dairy-free Bread

Preparation Time: 5 minutes
Cook Time: 2 hours 10 minutes
Servings: 1 loaf, 2.98 lb, 4.25 cups, 1296g

Ingredients:

- apple cider vinegar - 1 1/2 Tbsp (22g)
- Sugar- 2 tsp (8.4g)
- active dry yeast - 2 tsp (8.4g)
- egg white, room temperature- 1
- eggs, room temperature - 2
- olive oil - 4 1/2 Tbsp (75g)
- warm water - 1 1/2 cup (320ml)
- multi-purpose gluten-free flour- 3 1/3 cup (360g)

Preparation:

1. In a sizable mixing bowl, combine the warm water, sugar, and yeast; stir to combine. Set aside for 8 to 10 minutes, or until frothy.
2. In a different mixing dish, whisk together the two eggs and one egg white before adding to the bread machine baking pan.
3. To the baking pan, add oil and apple cider vinegar. Baking pan with frothy yeast/water mixture added.
4. On top, sprinkle the all-purpose gluten-free flour.
5. Start with the gluten-free bread setting.
6. Take out the bread from the baking pan, and invert it onto a cooling rack. Before slicing to serve, let the bread cool fully.

Nutritional facts:

Calories: 241, Fat: 6g, Carbs: 41g, Protein: 4g, Sugar: 2g, Potassium: 89mg, Sodium: 164mg

18.14 Cheese & Herb Bread

Preparation Time: 5 minutes
Cook Time: 1 hour |
Servings: 1 loaf, 2.92 lb, 3.61 cups, 1130g

Ingredients:

- dried basil - ¾ tsp (3.7g)
- dried oregano - ¾ tsp (3.7g)
- warm water - 300ml (1 ¼ cups)
- egg whites – 2
- grated Parmesan cheese- 2 Tbsp (30g)
- olive oil - 60ml (¼ cups)
- dried marjoram- 1 tsp (5g)
- Xanthan Gum - 2 tsp (8.4g)
- Salt- 1 tsp (5g)
- baking powder- 1/2 tsp (2.84g)
- gluten-free almond flour / or any other gluten-free flour, levelled - 200g (2 cups)
- apple cider vinegar- 1 Tbsp (15g)
- granulated sugar - 2 Tbsp (30g)
- dry active yeast- 7g (2 tsp)
- Tapioca/potato starch, levelled - 100g (1 cup)

Preparation:

1. According to your bread machine manufacturer, place all the ingredients into the bread machine's greased pan, and select a basic cycle / standard cycle/bake / quick bread / white bread setting. Then choose crust color, either medium or light, and press start to bake bread.
2. In the last kneading cycle, check the dough
3. it should be wet but thick, not like traditional bread dough. If the dough is too wet, put more flour, 1 Tbsp at a time, or until dough slightly firm.
4. When the cycle is finished and the machine turns off, remove baked bread from pan and cool on wire rack.

Nutritional facts: Calories: 150, Fat: 3g, Carbs: 9g, Protein: 4g, Sugar: 2g, Potassium: 76mg, Sodium: 415mg

18.15 Gluten-free Oat & Honey Bread

Preparation Time: 5 minutes
Cook Time: 3 hours

Servings: 1 loaf, 2.93 lb, 3.73 cups, 1318g

Ingredients:

- warm water - 1 1/4 cup (295ml)
- eggs – 2
- honey - 3 Tbsp (42g)
- gluten-free oats - 1 1/4 cup (260g)
- butter, melted - 3 Tbsp (42g)
- potato starch- 1/2 cup (100g)
- brown rice flour- 1 1/4 cup (260g)
- sugar - 1 1/2 tsp (6.4g)
- xanthan gum- 2 tsp (8.4g)
- active dry yeast - 1 1/2 Tbsp (22g)
- salt - 3/4 tsp

Preparation:

1. Except for the yeast, add the ingredients in the above-mentioned order.
2. The yeast should be placed in the center of the dry ingredients.
3. Press Start after selecting the gluten-free cycle and a light crust color.
4. Before cutting the bread to serve, remove it from the oven and let it cool for 20 minutes on a cooling rack.

Nutritional facts:

Calories: 151, Fat: 4g, Carbs: 27g, Protein: 6g, Sugar: 2g, Potassium: 67mg, Sodium: 265mg

18.16 Gluten-free Potato Bread

Preparation Time: 5 minutes
Cook Time: 3 hours

Servings: 1 loaf, 2.93 lb, 3.73 cups, 1407g

Ingredients:

- medium russet potato, baked, 1 or mashed leftovers
- honey - 3 Tbsp (42g)
- gluten-free quick yeast - 2 packets
- eggs,2
- warm almond milk- 3/4 cup (150ml)
- egg white - 1
- tapioca flour- 3/4 cup (150g)
- almond flour- 3 2/3 cup (467g)
- dried chives - 1 tsp (5g)
- sea salt- 1 tsp (5g)
- olive oil - 1/4 cup (21g)
- apple cider vinegar - 1 Tbsp (15g)

Preparation:

1. In a sizable mixing bowl, combine all of the dry ingredients with the exception of the yeast; set aside.
2. In a different mixing bowl, combine the honey, apple cider, oil, eggs and milk.
3. Fill the bread machine with the wet ingredients.
4. Over the wet components, layer the dry ingredients.
5. Add the yeast to the dry ingredients after making a well in them.
6. Press Start while selecting the gluten free bread setting and a light crust color.
7. Prior to slicing, let it cool completely.

Nutritional facts:

Calories: 232, Fat: 13g, Carbs: 17g, Protein: 4g, Sugar: 3g, Potassium: 67mg, Sodium: 173mg

19 CONVERSION TABLE

Measuring Equivalent Chart

3 tsp (15g)	**1 Tbsp (15g)**
2 Tbsp (30g)	1 ounce
4 tbsp (56g)	¼ cups (59g)
8 tbsp	½ cup (100g)
16 tbsp	1 cup (130g)
2 cups (240g)	1 pint
4 cups (544g)	1 quart
4 quarts	1 gallon

Type	Imperial	Imperial	Metric
Weight	1 dry ounce		28g
	1 pound	16 dry ounces	0.45 kg
	1 tsp (5g)		5 ml
	1 dessert spoon	2 tsp (8.4g)	10 ml
	1 Tbsp (15g)	3 tsp (15g)	15 ml
	1 Australian tbsp	4 tsp	20 ml
Volume	1 fluid ounce	2 Tbsp (30g)	30 ml
	1 cup (130g)	16 tbsp	240 ml
	1 cup (130g)	8 fluid ounces	240 ml
	1 pint	2 cups (240g)	470 ml
	1 quart	2 pints	0.95 l
	1 gallon	4 quarts	3.8 l
Length	1 inch		2.54 cm

* Numbers are rounded to the closest equivalent

Gluten-Free – Conversion Tables

All-Purpose Flour	Rice Flour	Potato Starch	Tapioca	Xanthan Gum
½ cup (100g)	1/3 cup (113g)	2 Tbsp (30g)	1 Tbsp (15g)	¼ tsp (8.4g)
1 cup (130g)	½ cup (100g)	3 Tbsp (42g)	1 Tbsp (15g)	1/2 tsp (2.84g)
¼ cups (59g)	¾ cup (150g)	1/3 cup (113g)	3 Tbsp (42g)	2/3 tsp (15g)
1 ½ cup (100g)	1 cup (130g)	5 Tbsp (70g)	3 Tbsp (42g)	2/3 tsp (15g)
1 ¾ cup (150g)	1 ¼ cups (59g)	5 Tbsp (70g)	3 Tbsp (42g)	1 tsp (5g)
2 cups (240g)	1 ½ cup (100g)	1/3 cup (113g)	1/3 cup (113g)	1 tsp (5g)
2 ½ cup (354g)	1 ½ cup (100g)	½ cup (100g)	¼ cups (59g)	1 1/8 tsp
2 2/3 cup (227g)s	2 cups (240g)	½ cup (100g)	¼ cups (59g)	1 ¼ tsp (8.4g)
3 cups (360g)	2 cups (240g)	2/3 cup (227g)	1/3 cup (113g)	1 ½ cup (100g)

Flour: quantity and weight

Flour Amount (cup)	Flour Amount (grams)
1	**140**
3/4	**105**
1/2	**70**
1/4	**35**

Sugar: quantity and weight

Sugar Amount (cup)	SugarFlour Amount (grams)
1	200
3/4	150
2/3	135
1/2	100
1/3	70
1/4	50

Powdered Sugar Amount (cup)	Powdered SugarFlour Amount (grams)
1	160
3/4	120
1/2	80
1/4	40

Cream Amount (cup)	Cream Amount (ml)	Cream Amount (grams)
1	250	235
3/4	188	175
1/2	125	115
1/4	63	60
1 tbsp.	15	15

Butter: quantity and weight

Butter Amount)
1 cup (130g) = 8 ounces = 2 sticks = 16 tbsp =230 grams
1/2 cup (100g) = 4 ounces = 1 stick = 8 tbsp = 115 grams
¼ cups (59g) = 2 ounces = ½ stick = 4 tbsp (56g)= 58 grams

Oven Temperature Equivalent Chart

Fahrenheit (°F)	Celsius(°C)	Gas Mark
220	100	
225	110	1/4
250	120	1/2
275	140	1
300	150	2
325	160	3
350	180	4
375	190	5
400	200	6
425	220	7
450	230	8
475	250	9
500	260	

* Celsius (°C) = T (°F)-32] * 5/9

**Fahrenheit (°F) = T (°C) * 9/5 + 32

*** Numbers are rounded to the closest equivalent

20 CONCLUSION

This book has introduced you to an array of simple yet delectable bread recipes. A common challenge for individuals adhering to a diet is the necessity to eliminate many beloved foods, particularly those high in sugar or carbohydrates such as bread. This cookbook aims to address this issue by offering alternatives. It is essential to adopt a positive mindset. Adhering to a balanced diet can contribute to the prevention of diabetes, heart disease, and respiratory ailments. Moreover, if you are already experiencing issues associated with these conditions, following a diet under medical supervision can significantly ameliorate your health. The bread recipes in this book utilize commonplace ingredients readily available at local stores, eliminating the need to seek specialty shops or place orders online. These breads enable you to indulge in your favorite dishes while maintaining adherence to your dietary goals. Savor the taste of freshly baked bread with your preferred toppings and fulfill your cravings without compromising your health.

Additionally, this book underscores the significance of the bread machine as an indispensable asset in your kitchen. Operating a bread machine is not daunting; familiarize yourself with its features and functions. Regular use will help you understand the intricacies and best practices. It is crucial to meticulously read the user manual that accompanies your bread machine, as it contains invaluable information regarding the proper loading of ingredients, settings, and maintenance. Note that instructions may vary based on the make and model of your bread machine. Devoting time to comprehending the manual will equip you with the knowledge necessary to maximize the efficiency of your bread machine, yielding optimal results.

The bread machine is a boon for both seasoned bakers and novices. This versatile appliance facilitates the production of bread with impeccable texture and flavor with minimal effort. Bread-making is an art that requires precision and finesse, particularly when handling different types of flour. The bread machine empowers you to master this art, irrespective of your level of expertise.

In this cookbook, we have delved into the essentials of bread machines, their utilization, and maintenance. We have also provided insights into the primary ingredients of bread, such as flour and yeast, and discussed the variations necessary for producing different types of bread. Furthermore, an assortment of scrumptious bread recipes is presented for you to experiment with at home.

BONUS: As a token of appreciation, scan the QR code below to access nine fantastic bonuses. Simply provide your email and leave an honest review of my book on Amazon. You will receive four mobile apps featuring bread machine recipes, one mobile app to calculate your daily caloric intake, and four online courses on bread machines.

LINK: https://BookHip.com/TCCGLWH

Printed in Great Britain
by Amazon

25977912R00051